Coastlines of ITALY

This volume is part of a series of volumes on Coastlines of the World. The papers included in the volume are to be presented at Coastal Zone '89.

Volume edited by Paolo Fabri
Series edited by Orville T. Mago

D0071499

Published by the
American Society of Civil Engineers
345 East 47th Street
New York, New York 10017-2398

ABSTRACT

These papers were presented at Coastal Zone '89 the Sixth Symposium on Coastal and Ocean Management held in Charleston, South Carolina, July 11-14, 1989. This volume is a part of a series of volumes on Coastlines of the World. Some of the topics covered include conservation policies, coastal pollution, erosional trends, use of the sea for leisure, and the historical evolution of coastal Italy. This volume provides the civil engineer with a broad understanding of coastal and ocean management issues related to the coastlines of Italy.

Library of Congress Cataloging-in-Publication Data

Coastlines of Italy.
     p.   cm.—(Coastlines of the world series)
    Includes index.
    ISBN 0-87262-706-3
    1. Coasts—Italy.   2. Shore protection—Italy.   I. American Society of Civil Engineers.   II. Series.
333.91'7'0945—dc20   89-14922
                                    CIP

FOREWORD

Coastal Zone '89, a major American Society of Civil Engineers (ASCE) Specialty Conference, was the sixth in a series of multidisciplinary meetings on comprehensive coastal and ocean management. Professionals, citizens and decision makers met for four days in Charleston, South Carolina to exchange information and views on matters ranging from regional to international in scope and interest. This year's theme was entitled "Spotlight on Solutions", emphasizing a recurrent focus on practical problem solving.

Other sponsors and affiliates besides ASCE included the National Oceanic and Atmospheric Space Administration, the American Shore and Beach Preservation Association, Department of Commerce, the Coastal Zone Foundation and many other organizations (see title page). The range of sponsorship hints at the diversity of those attending. The presence of viewpoints will surely stimulate improved coastal and ocean management through the best of current knowledge and cooperation.

This volume is part of the "Coastlines of the World" series produced in conjunction with the Coastal Zone '89 Conference. The purpose of this special regional volume is to focus on one geographical area in depth.

Each volume of the "Coastlines of the World" series will have a guest series editor representing the particular geographical area of interest discussed in that volume.

All papers have been accepted for publication by the Proceedings Editors. All papers are eligible for discussion in the Journal of Waterway, Port, Coastal and Ocean Engineering and all papers are eligible for ASCE Awards.

A seventh conference is now being planned to maintain this dialogue and information exchange. Information is available through the Coastal Zone Foundation, P.O. Box 26062, San Francisco, CA 94126, USA.

Orville T. Magoon
Series Editor

ITALIANS AND THEIR COASTAL ZONE:
AN INTRODUCTION TO SOME PECULIARITIES

Paolo Fabbri*

Any map of the area makes Italy appear as a coastal and maritime country: a long peninsula, stretching from the core of Europe down to the middle of the Mediterranean, where two major islands—Sicily and Sardinia—and a good number of minor ones seem to scatter all around the influence of Italian culture and political strategies.

However, this is a geographical trick. At least twice in the past it gave to Italians the vision of the Mediterranean as a *mare nostrum*, "our own sea", but neither time did this approach prove correct. It was actually correct in Roman times, when the whole basin was tightly unified for a few centuries under a unique rule, the *imperium*. But modern Italians—that is, the people that started to perceive its own national identity at least one millennium after the fall of the empire and finally became a nation in the 1800s—this people cannot be assimilated with ancient Romans.

Truly indeed, over the centuries that have elapsed, Italian city-states as Venice, Genoa and, for a short period, Pisa, have played a major role in Mediterranean affairs, especially in trading: but they were not the only ones.

In approaching the Mediterranean as a medium for overseas expansion or a ground for the practice of piracy, Greeks and Byzantines, Turks and Arabs have gone much further than Italians and other European peoples.

In the 7th to 11th century and again in the 1500s up to the 1700s, Italy was practically under siege of pirate fleets based in North Africa and the Levant and over a thousand of coastal watch-towers—a good part of them still in existence—could not prevent dozens of successful landings, ending up with bloody plunders and deportations. Only the northern shores on both sides of the peninsula could be regarded as relatively safe, being the farthest for the pirate reach and the closest to the protection of Venetian and Genoese navies: nonetheless, around 1550 the town of Rapallo, just 15 miles from Genoa, was sacked and destroyed.

As a contribution to this volume points out, up to the 1800s most of Italian flat coastlands were marshy and affected with malaria: the city of Venice and other minor villages lying on flat coasts did survive because of their locations in lagoons, where tidal movements prevent marshes and keep the environment clear of malaria. Short stretches of cliffy coasts did encourage settlement, because of the presence of small and well sheltered harbor sites, mostly used for local fishing; but as a rule rugged morphology has not proven to be a factor favouring settlement, nor farming activities.

---
*Professor of Political Geography at the University of Bologna, Italy; Secretary of the Commission on the Coastal Environment of the International Geographical Union. Address: University of Bologna, Via Zamboni, 38, Bologna 40126, Italy.

When piracy faded away as a result of the impact with the guns of modern navies, these navies took over complete control of the Mediterranean: the British, the French, the Austro-Hungarian, not the Italian. Italy was not a unified nation yet and in fact the land itself was under the control or the direct rule of these Europeans powers. An Italian navy was put together after political unification, in the 1860s: it developed and gained its portion of importance, limited to the Mediterranean, up to the Second World War. This was the other moment when Italians, pressed by national feelings, felt the Mediterranean as *mare nostrum*, their own sea: it lasted shortly however.

Italy entered the war boasting one of the most powerful navies in the world: it included eight modern battleships, over fifty submarines and a great number of cruisers and destroyers. With the exceptions of a few submarines, it never operated seriously outside the Mediterranean and never got control even of its own territorial waters. Many good reasons explain such an unsuccessful performance: submarines were slow and imprecise in shooting torpedoes and their armours were extremely thin; battleships could hardly operate because of lack of escort ships and fuel: most of them were sunk while in port. The war brought to an end all Italian hopes of being a major maritime country.

The present Italian navy is regarded as rather efficient; but it is a minor one, operating within NATO strategies. The commercial fleet has gone through a very rapid recovery after the war, but its turnover and renewal are heavily hampered by shipyards difficulties. The fishing fleet also enjoyed redevelopment and modernization in the 1950s, but is now steadily decreasing. Although many Italians love fishing as a leisure activity (mainly practised on land), the number of those who got to dislike professional fishing has been steadily increasing over recent years.

Indeed Italians love sea food and it used to be a popular practice over the last decades to have day-trips to the coast with the basic aim of a sea food dinner. A huge number of restaurants specialized in sea food has now been established in all inland areas, in large cities as in the farming countryside, to meet this excess of demand. They all turn into good business, as well as the thousands traditionally located along coast. By far the larger portion of the food consumed however, is imported: seas surrounding Italy abound in mullets and mackerels, sardines and anchovies, cods and tunnies, but these fishes are not very popular and unlike to be served in restaurants: therefore they have a limited market, which also explains the decrease in commercial fishing. Instead, restaurants offer soles and turbots, salmons and cuts of shark, shrimps and prawns, lobsters and scallops and most of these are imported from all continents. It is questionable whether the choices of the public have driven this tendency to import, or the opposite. But the fact remains that Italians find it easier to import sea food than to harvest their own, thus showing a diffused lack of knowledge and confidence with their marine environment, which could be the result of a long-recorded relationship, based on fears and hostility.

The recent boom of pleasure boating, also illustrated in a couple of articles of this volume, does not appear to be contradictory to these feelings. On considering the generally small sizes of these boats, the use of them—limited to waters very close to the coast and to calm seas, clear skies and warm days—and the fact that many look fit for parties to be held at their mooring-berths rather than for sailing, it is suggested that pleasure boats are regarded more as symbols of a social status than tools for navigating and acquiring a more confident perception of the open sea.

It goes by itself that this attitude of the Italians towards the sea is generic but not general. The country boasts a very brilliant record in sea trading, although it has been gradually fading after the age of discoveries (i.e. in the last five centuries), when the Mediterranean lost its supremacy. Notwithstanding the marginality of the position with respect to the world network of sea routes, Italy still plays an important role in sea transportation. This does not imply however, strong and diffused feelings for sea-faring: modern freighters, even large ones, only need small crews.

Italian coasts show a high density of harbours of all sizes and for all uses: many of them look totally or partially obsolete or even abandoned, but this is a familiar look to many countries and to be related to the present period of rapid changes in sea transportation. What seems peculiar of Italy however, is the relatively weak tie between the harbour and the city (or the town or the village) both in connecting structures and in cultural approaches. An aspect of this is the obsolence of many urban waterfronts, as well as the physical barriers between the harbour area and the city. This is not always true: the diffusion of turism has turned many fishing villages into resorts, where old and new values and functions nicely blend together along the waterfront promenade. In many other cases however, the traditional setting of the waterfront has been smashed by massive building schemes, which have encouraged a front line location of banks, offices, high-rated hotels and high-revenue residents, thus pushing back social groups which had been linked to the sea for generations.

Hardly 3 million people lived within a few miles from the shoreline at the turn of the century, mostly clustered in old and densely populated centres which had experienced in past centuries profound feelings of interest and fear towards the sea. At present, coastal population totals over 10 million people, with most of the increase resulting from immigration from inland areas. Few countries in the world and none in Europe have gone through a parallel growth of population and new settlement along their coastal areas. Agriculture in newly reclaimed lands and seaside attraction for tourism have been the major factors of this peculiarity.

Although widely experienced in the previous four centuries, large reclamation schemes met definite success only in the period 1890–1960, when sufficient energy became available for the lifting of water from marshy lowlands, partially below sea level; and when the central government undertook part of the financial burden of the operation. Malaria affected hundreds of thousands of people and it had become a serious social problem; also, new land was badly needed for an increasing population, mostly devoted to agriculture. Along coastal lowlands, reclamation gave way to new patterns of sparse settlement, including roads, and improved or created totally new accesses to long and wide stretches of sunny and sandy beaches.

This paved the way to coastal tourism and recreation, for which Italy has represented the top choice for Europeans in the years between 1930 and 1970. Over this period, among Mediterranean countries (the best vocated in the continent for seaside tourism, on account of their mild climate), Italy had the very best offer: not as high in class as the French Blue Coast, but not as developed either and so much cheaper; on the other hand, largely superior in facilities and more accessible than any of the other riparian countries. This splendid and varied offer, finely complemented by high-rated sceneries and unique historical and artistic values, successfully met an unprecedented demand, both foreign and domestic, and the mixture was an explosive one. More than elsewhere, tourism has been profitable to long-settled as well as newly immigrated coastal populations, but unpleasant to the landscape and the environment. As a result, it is going to be in the short run unpleasant for populations to.

This leads to consider another peculiarity of Italian coastlands, i.e. the areal extension of the development schemes, both along shore and beaches. Indeed, massive and messy and unplanned coastal development is a common feature of all countries, originating from cultural and economic processes which have been largely similar to Italy's. In this country the difference is basically a matter of quantity: recent and heavy coastal development lines up with no relevant discontinuity for hundreds of miles. With the exception of a few spots with difficult access, mainly in the Po delta, all coastal plains are developed and high, cliffy coasts are not in a better shape, especially in the North.

High offer and high demand for coastal recreation are rather ubiquitous in the world and do not seem sufficient reasons to explain Italian peculiarities. Other processes should be taken into account. Since the end of Second World War, the needs of reconstruction stimulated the establishing of numerous building contractors, employing over one million of people. When, after a decade, the reconstruction was over, this huge labour force could hardly be demobilized, as hundreds of thousands of workers shifting to other industrial sectors—mainly mechanical, chemical and car-making—and to service activities, were being replaced by others, migrating from the under-developed farming areas in the South and in other mountain districts. This excess of supply in constructions was partly met by public works (new auto-roads, harbour structures, urban expansion, industries, agricultural settlement in reclaimed areas) and partly induced the supply of new houses to stimulate the demand, thus encouraging the construction of secondary homes in areas vocated for tourism or recreation. Whether they have or not a cultural tendency towards owning secondary homes, Italians do use such kind of accommodation in their leisure time more than any other European people; and they do prefer them to other kinds of accommodation, as hotels, campings or caravans. Secondary homes are mostly used for a month per year or even for a few week-ends. Their cost therefore is not worth their use: not only from a private standpoint but also for the public, which bears most of the urbanizing costs related to the presence of a house.

As to Italian beaches, in general they are not more crowded on top season than other countries': but they do look more densely used on account of the wide range of beach facilities and equipment which they present and this is still another peculiarity, which should be briefly explained. All beaches are a property of the central government, which leases sectors of them to entrepreneurs. The number of these is not supplied by official sources, but a rough evaluation accounts for 50 to 70 thousands: each of them constructs on the beach a *bagno* (beach house or bath house) some times simple, some others provided with all possible facilities, including restaurants, coffeeshops, skating and volley-ball grounds, video-games. Hundreds of umbrellas, tents, deck-chairs are placed between the *bagno* and the shoreline and quite often beach users pay for access. This forms up a big business, mostly satisfying a domestic demand: as other Mediterraneans, Italians like to be close enough to everyday facilities when they spend their time on the beach and here they tend to prefer the shade to the sun. Foreigners don't dislike this kind of offer, however they tend to privilege open beaches, where they can sun-bathe better.

In such conditions, any problem deriving from shore-line erosion or even to a temporary retreat tends to be in Italy more serious than elsewhere. Even a minor storm, which would be harmless to an open beach, can damage costly equipment and give way to bitter protest and complaints on part of the managers of the *bagni*. This usually brings to the construction of costly artificial structures, which are paid for by the central government, and do constitute a major factor in deteriorating the standards of coastal waters, where users should bathe.

Never mind, as long as the business circuit can continue: thousands of pleasure boats, fresh-water swimming pools, waste disposals and sewage plants are constructed every year along Italian coastal areas. They are all means either to try and improve water quality or to escape from bathing practices. Coastal business also go through other unsuspected paths, related to the post-industrial age: thousands of planners make plans for local governments which are never implemented; many more environmentalists earn a living through talking and writing on how the environment is spoiled; hundreds of biologists sample coastal waters to check if they comply to EEC regulations; dozens of lawyers study ways through which the government should ask for a postponment to comply with the same regulations. This draws to a conclusion as to the main peculiarity of the Italian coastal zone. Yes: it is a big business.

CONTENTS

*Manuscript not available at the time of printing.

SESSION 56: AESTHETIC, CULTURAL, AND HISTORICAL PERSPECTIVES

SESSION 71: SHORELINE VARIATIONS: MEDITERRANEAN AND WEST AFRICAN STUDIES

POSTER SESSION

PAPERS AT LARGE

*Manuscript not available at the time of printing.

COASTAL PLANNING AND CONSERVATION POLICIES IN ITALY

PIETRO MARIO MURA*

Abstract: The evolution of coastal planning and the implementation of conservation policies in Italy have been conditioned by the scant awareness of the problems concerning coastal areas, by the setting up of "regioni" and by the fragmentariness and superimposition of administrative competences. Therefore, only limited results have been achieved in the field of nature parks and reserves. Better results are hoped to be obtained from laws and other planning regulations -enacted in the Eighties by the State and regions- concerning landscape plans and the plan for the defence of the sea and the marine coast against pollution.

Introduction

The problem of coastal planning has been only recently a matter for scientific and political debate in Italy. In fact, only in the Seventies were the first real signs recognised of the awareness of the gravity and urgency of some problems emerging from the coastal areas; however without underlining the specificity of the coastal zone with respect to the other fields planning activity can be applied to. It is possible to start from this observation to understand the piece-meal and episodic actions adopted in the field (both with reference to the geographical and sectorial aspect) and their non-integration into a single territorial frame of reference (Pranzini E., 1985).

The stimulus towards public interventions, even if sectorial in nature and not specifically aimed at the needs of coastal areas, stems from three main problems, closely concerned with the environment:
- the worsening of the environmental conditions because of the spreading and intensifying of pollution sources, both seaward and landward;

---

* Faculty of Architecture, University of Reggio Calabria
   Via Cimino, 2 - 89125 Reggio Calabria, Italy

1

- the consequent growing menace to the survival of marine ecosystems and the feedback of negative effects on coastal areas;
- the stimulus provided by international and EEC agreements to face pollution (Fiorelli F., 1988; United Nations, 1982).

Which are some of the causes for delay in understanding these problems and coping with them?

The delay in scientific formulation

The delay in the field of territorial sciences in reaching suitable conceptualization of the "coastal zone", is surely one of the principal causes.

This delay is to be attributed, on one hand to the lack of a suitable methodology, able to master the complexity and the interdependence of the processes responsible for the organisation of the coastal areas; on the other hand to the fact that organisational and management problems of the territory have been mainly approached from a "landward" point of view. Furthermore, in the Italian experience, the effects of sea management on the mainland have received scant attention (Vallega A., 1988; Zunica M., 1986).

The "Preliminary Report to the National Economic Program 1971/75", better known as "Progetto '80", can be considered as the cultural source of current formulations.

The interest in such a document does not stem from the fact that it contains planning guidelines for coastal areas, but rather because it assumes a systematic approach to the problems of conservation, protection and exploitation of the physical environment and natural resources, which include the littorals (the concept of coastal zone is never taken into consideration), even by the institution of parks and nature reserves. The "Progetto '80" does not go further (Min. Bilancio Progr. Econ., 1969).

One of the first attempts to face systematically the study of the coast has been made by ENEL (the National Agency for Energy), which has carried out wide research with the aim of building up a data base for each region, from which to get information about the many features of a territory and to better define the location of its own power stations.

The coast is depicted as a land belt, parallel to the sea, whose width varies according to the boundaries of the "comuni", within which the geomorphologic features, the organisation, the planning situation, the demographic characteristics and the development indicators that are considered their primary characteristic, are analysed using a systematic approach.

However, the strategic reference is made to a belt of 30 kms inland, within which only the principal components of territorial organisation (settlements, transport networks, rivers, etc.) are considered. The altimetrical profile is developped 3 kms inland from the water edge, with particular emphasis as far as 0,5 km, while also a belt of sea is considered as far as the -10 m. bathymetric line and the presence of ports is registered, because of their direct interest for the location of power stations.

In spite of its attitude, the study carried out by ENEL takes the sea into consideration only marginally, notwithstanding the awareness of the impact that power stations have on it (water drawing, thermal pollution, fuel leakages, etc.)(ENEL, 1973).

A significant improvement towards the formulation of a modern concept of the coastal zone (with its operative implications) was made, nearly contemporarily with the above mentioned study, in a new study carried out by the ISPE, concerning the organisation of Italian coastal areas. Such a study goes beyond the view of the coast as a belt of emerged land defined in terms of its closeness to the sea (a sort of boundary-frontier between two different spaces); it moves towards the definition as a belt of the earth's surface covering both emerged and submerged zones, in each of which the kind of political and economic organisation is conditioned by the presence of and the contiguity of one with the other (Min. Bilancio Progr. Econ., 1974).

This attitude, which reflects a geographical inspiration, remained isolated. The "territorial culture" was not able to grasp its methodological and operative implications. The main reason for such a difficulty stems from the functional and rationalist approach, based on zoning, typical of the present legislation and from the fragmentariness and superimposition of competences they bring (as it will be better seen later) (Landini and Mura, 1982).

It is precisely in the geographical field, thanks to the studies of Vallega, that a deeper insight into both the method and the contents of coastal areas is maturing.

Vallega starts from the consideration that in the coastal zone -an environment of such unstable ecological equilibria- the tensions produced by the introduction of both new structures and new functions brought about by economic and technological impulses, often of universal importance and operating at different scales, are intensely felt (Vallega A., 1980, 1985).

The effects of this situation is shown by the many and complex organisational forms that can be found in these spaces and that can be summarised in coastal zone and coastal region. The latter is a special space because it encompasses two environments: the sea and the land, very

different from each other, where both integrated forms of
occupation and exploitation of resources can be observed,
under   the   pressure   exerted   by   processes   which
contemporarily involve both the land and the sea. These
processes bring about feedbacks in part very different and
more complex, than the ones that can be observed in inland
areas, whose boundaries tend to coincide with the area in
which they operate.

    The complexity of "spontaneous" organisational forms
contrasts with the spatial forms set up by the law which
aims to accomodate, rather late, the increase in the number
of uses to which the coastal areas are put (increase of the
need for protection and conservation; growth of links and
conflicts among different uses, involvement and integration
of ever larger spaces, etc.) (Vallega A., 1988).

    Also outside the geographical field the awareness of
the relevant operative implication of such a position has
gained   credit,   notwithstanding   the   lack   of   a   deep
methodological   insight.   However,   the   difficulty   of
translating   wide   and   complex   problems   concerning
territorial   organisation   into   effective   plans   appeared
evident; this has entailed a sectorial and limited
approach, mainly by the public authority (Karrer F., 1984,
1986).

    In fact, the technical problems involved are more
complex than it is possible to guess at a first glance,
since they pose at least three questions:
1) the supposed peculiarity of "coastal planning" within
the field of planning "tout court";
2) the geographical area of reference, which can vary
remarkably according to whether we refer to coastal
planning or to regional coastal planning;
3) the choice of the subject responsible for this kind of
planning (the "regione" is the most suitable administrative
level, but does not have complete powers)(Gabrielli B.,
1988).

Institutional and administrative planning competences

    The delay in adapting to new needs the instruments and
the techniques for planning and managing coastal areas
depends   also   on   the   distribution   of   ruling   and
administrative competence concerning planning (DOCTER,
1986).

    As already shown, in the Italian experience, a set of
rules particularly aimed at coastal areas is absent. The
law regulates planning "tout court", which is devolved to
the regions and has to be exerted within the principles set
out by the national Parliament. However, other public
bodies have administrative competences, so that the
competences on the coastal areas, belonging to many public

bodies at different hierarchical levels (comuni, regioni, State) overlap. Furthermore national competences are split among Ministries; consequently it is almost impossible to envisage management of the coastal areas under a sole authority.

The main administrative competence belongs to the "comuni" so that (lacking general rules originating from the regioni on a large scale to refer to) the territorial situation seems much like a mosaic whose pieces do not fit.

We have also to take into consideration that a wide part of important functions concerning the organisation and management of coastal areas belongs to national Ministries:
- the Ministry of Mercantile Marine has competence in sea navigation, in the use of both the sea and the beaches (maritime state property) and in sea fishery;
- the Ministry of Industry has, among others, competence in the field of research and extraction of fossil fuels (also both in territorial waters and on the continental shelf), to authorize power stations and energy distribution plants;
- the Ministry of Public Works has competence in urban planning, hydraulic works, use of public waters, sewage systems, aqueducts, etc.;
- the Ministry of Beni Culturali has competence in the field of amenities of historical and artistic interest and of nature beauty;
- the Ministry of Environment (established in 1983) has competence as far as protection against pollution is concerned;
- other Ministries have competence in military defence, hydraulic land reclamation, etc..

The evolution of the rules concerning and the plans to protect areas of natural beauty

Notwithstanding the fragmentation and the overlapping of competences exposed above, coastal areas have been the object of many sectorial laws which, even if they do not provide consistent and satisfactorily solutions to their needs in the fields of organisation, protection and conservation, give partial answers to many of the problems up for discussion.

The delay and the fragmentation of competences have brought delay and shortcomings as far as the implementation and the management of plans are concerned.

Up to the enactment of the act on town planning n. 1150/1942 (which is mainly concerned with the organisation and development of building activity in settlements, and so with conflicting interests pertinent to different uses of the land) the only source of regulation was the special act n. 1497/1939 for the "Protection of natural beauties and the landscape". The coast is not included as such, but only in so far as the conditions regulated by the law occur there: the existence of either rare or exceptional qualities (natural beauty, landscape, geologic sites, etc.). The only aim of the law is the preservation of the external appearance (the aesthetic of the landscape), imposing constraints on the right to build, without an evaluation of the economic and social processes responsible for the organisation of coastal areas.

The set of plans approved covers two different time spans. In the first, from the approval of the above mentioned act up to the implementation of regional organisation, only 14 plans have been approved, most of them concerning coastal areas (AA.VV., 1986).

Their scant number and the very small land surface involved (from the barely 6 hectares in the plan for Osimo to nearly 3000 in the one for Versilia) does not allow these plans to play a particularly meaningful role in the organisation of coastal areas. Also the plan for Portofino (the first, having been approved in 1935, and among the most important), managed by a special body, the "Ente Autonomo del Monte di Portofino", concerns a belt of one km inland, parallel to the coastline (which includes the whole comune of Portofino and part of Camogli and Santa Margherita Ligure) where shooting and picking rare plant species are forbidden and a preventive authorisation is needed to make even the slightest transformation of the territory.

Other plans have been drawn up as simple detail plans and they have been absorbed into the planning instruments of the comuni, subsequently approved (e.g. Nervi, Sperlonga, Versilia, Argentario). The need to protect the landscape seems to go along with the needs of economic development only episodically and marginally (e.g. Procida).

One of the most limiting aspects of such plans (apart from the reference to building activities and their application planning constraints by the authorities) has been the poor support provided by the basic scientific analysis contained, which should underpin the planning regulations.

Moreover the results were no better, in the Sixties, for the plans prepared for 29 tourist development areas in the South, defined by Cassa per il Mezzogiorno and including large structures of coastal areas which got no further than the study stage.

More hopeful signs of a deeper insight into the problems of the territory (and therefore also of the coastal areas) seem visible in other landscape plans, but unfortunately they too remained at the study stage (east coast of provincia of Nuoro, Campi Flegrei, Costiera Amalfitana, Penisola Sorrentina, Comprensorio Trulli and

Grotte).

These plans vary considerably because of the large areas of land involved (in the case of Nuoro a belt of land 170 kms long and 1 km landward) and because of the constraints imposing public use only on a belt parallel to the coastline (from 150 to 250 m. and sometimes more, excludind areas already under private use, again in the case of Nuoro). But, what is more important for the aims we are concerned with, these studies are based on the analysis and recognition of ecological components in the landscape (landscape and ecosystems). The aim of the plans is in fact to protect "natural beauties" considered from the point of view of their balance with them and human activities.

The setting up of the regions has gone aside with the beginning of a new phase characterised by the emergence of a new culture better adapted to the complexity of the coastal areas (in the wider context of the territory in general) which comes to fruition more definitely in the Eighties. In this direction we can identify two lines of research which are closely connected.

The first is concerned with measures to protect coast and marine areas by the creation of parks and nature reserves (either as national or regional initiative). The second line of research is concerned with national and regional planning activity, both of a general nature and strategically aimed at coastal areas.

Parks and nature reserves

The setting up of parks and nature reserves has not affected the coastal areas to a large extent. Of the five national parks, intended to preserve areas of exceptional importance and natural complexity, of international interest, only one, the park of Circeo, includes coastal land. In this park, completely wild nature reserves guarantee absolute protection for the coastal ecosystems which are defined as wet areas of international importance according to the Ramsar Convention. In order to reinforce this situation, in 1979 the Lazio Region set up an oasis of external protection for the coastal lakes.

Of the 36 regional parks recently set up (if we except the park Paneveggio Pale of S. Martino in the Trentino A.A. region, set up in 1967, all the others have been created since 1974, after the setting up of the regions and mainly in the Eighties) only two in Tuscany include coastal areas: the parks of Maremma and Migliarino-San Rossore.

A very similar picture is offered by nature reserves (121 national reserves and about 20 regional ones): only a quarter of these involve coastal areas (TCI, 1982; Pinna M., 1984).

In the case of completely wild reserve they offer

interesting almost unchanged natural environments (like e.
g. Nordio wood in Veneto, Ruins of Circe in Lazio and the
lake of Varano in Puglia); where man's intervention is more
strongly felt (e.g. in the isle of Caprera) they offer
protection in order to supervise and orientate natural
evolution and finally to achieve specific sectorial aims
(e.g. the repopulation of wild life, of particular species
of trees, etc.). These reserves include about 20 wet
coastal areas considered of international importance and
several hundreds of biotopes.

The general picture which emerges is not very
encouraging especially if we consider that only very
recently has there been a significant increase in the
number and area of the reserves (between 1975 and 1977
their area has tripled increasing from 18.000 to 55.000
he); this increase has however been followed by a period of
inactivity. Furthermore the geographical distribution of
the areas which are protected and or subject to constraint
-which leaves without protected areas the large islands
(Sicily and Sardinia) and some regions with a long
coastline (e.g. Calabria) is a sufficient reliable
indicator of the absence, on one hand of an organic
reference plan and on the other hand of a widespread
understanding, especially among public administrators, of
the problems of the environment and particularly of the
coastal environment.

We can find clear evidence of this if we note that up
to 1976 existing regulations only referred to protection of
natural beauties and only in act n. 72/1975 (which in any
case refers to the economic support to mountain areas) is
reference made for the first time to nature conservation.

The new national and regional planning

A considerable progress towards a strategy of real
nature conservation was only made with the passing of act
n. 431/1985 which contains "urgent regulations for the
protection of the areas of particular environmental
interest" (AA.VV., 1986).

This act, as we have already seen, goes beyond mere
aestethic concepts based on the evolution of only external
and formal elements of the landscape; it defines as
deserving of protection areas and elements of the territory
chosen because of their physical characteristic objectively
analysed (and not as in the past on the basis of their
subjective evaluation), and recognise their structural
importance for the physical features and the organisation
of the national territory.

From the recognition of such basic principle stems the
policy that the environment must be the object of specific
regulations governing its use and enhancement to be

implemented by means of the drawing up by the regions of
territorial landscape plans. In absence of such plans rigid
constraints are placed on certain sections of the
territory, and among these land included in a belt of 300
m. starting from shoreline, also in the case of elevated
coastal areas.

For the first time protection is provided for entire
categories of natural amenities -and therefore for a large
part of the national territory-; these areas are recognised
as having primary importance as a real resource for
development, compared to any option for building and urban
transformation.

In practice the fail to adopt the territorial
landscape plan has caused (even if only temporarily) the
immobilisation of activity in the coastal belt (moreover it
is calculated that about 20% of the national territory is
subject to such constraint!).

The few territorial landscape plans which have
originated from this act contain useful references to the
coastal areas from the point of view of methodology and
organisation (e.g. in the plan for Lower Lazio) (Regione
Lazio, 1986). The existence is recognised of territorial
sub-systems within which the conservation of any part of
the territory is closely linked to its territorial
contexts. The coastal area is considered as a belt of
variable depth of which different types of landscapes are
analysed in order to preserve them.

However coastal planning must be carried out
considering this area in itself and through its
interactions with the rest of the territory (including an
evaluation of the coastal shelf considered implicitely as a
continuation of the dry land which is extended for a short
distance towards the open sea and very broken and rocky).

In the same general picture the most important plan is
the one drawn by Emilia-Romagna region (Regione Emilia
Romagna, 1986). The regulation of the plan -which aims at
achieving active conservation of the territory (and not
only the passive application of constraints), according to
a unified view of environment and territory- is organised
according to territorial systems (5 are identified) one of
which, the second largest, is the coastal system. In this
system four different areas are recognised, graded
according to the intensity of conservation. The definition
of coastal area contained in act n. 431/1985 is not
accepted; a definition drawn on the basis of morphological
and geographical observation with explicit reference to
regional regulations is preferred (regional acts n. 47/78
and n. 23/80) which measures the coast not from the
shoreline, but from the limit of the State property
("demanio"), so that the area subject to constraint is much
larger.

In other regional examples the recognition of the complex organisation of coastal areas (particularly because of the presence there of an articulated system of ports and because of the significant problems connected with reorganising the waterfront) has produced the singling out of regulations regarding the coast in order to include them in an autonomous coastal plan (not yet issued) (Regione Liguria, 1986)(1).

Regulations regarding the sea

The regions had started to gain interest to coastal areas (measured from the shoreline or from the "demanio" limit) at the beginning of the Seventies, by passing stop-gap acts preventing development in coastal areas, while awaiting the application of town planning regulations of the comuni.

We have already referred to the Emilia-Romagna region. Other regions have passed acts concerning belts parallel to the coast of variable depth (e.g. in Calabria 150 m. from the demanio).

These isolated measures (intended as an emergency) have never led to the drawing up of comprehensive plans. Only one region: Sicily, of particular significance because it is the largest Italian island, is putting through a regional plan for the protection of the littoral (Regione Siciliana, 1988).

The general aims of this plan can be summarised in three types:

1)- to achieve the decongestion of the coastal area by transferring inland activities not directly connected with the coast;

2)- to protect and preserve natural and landscape resources and reclaim land of environmental decay;

3)- to allow the natural fluctuation of the coastline by keeping free land adjacent to the shore.

The definition of coast has been based on the identification of geomorphological elements for many reasons:

- because of the explicit relationship between land and sea, in so far as beneath the surface the continuity of the geological structure implies close morphological and ecological links between the land and the sea environments;

-because these elements provide vital information for the knowledge of the territory as well as the substrate of the territorial transformation;

- because they can form the coastal aspect of further planning processes which concern inland territories.

The proposed plan identifies 19 geomorphological units and 21 areas for priority intervention regarding varied and multifaceted aspects:

- areas which have been particularly damaged by a high level of construction and creation of coastal infrastructure and of pollution (e.g. Milazzo, Cefalù and Castellammare del Golfo);
- areas of exceptional geomorphological interest (e.g. Capo d'Orlando, Trapani lagoon);
- areas subject to unplanned and fragmentary use (e.g. Capo d'Orlando, Termini Imerese);
- nature reserves to be expanded (e.g. the Marsala lagoon).

Finally, of particular importance is the recognition of the non-essentiality of building new marinas because of the delicate environmental state of the coast (in addition to reasons connected with the demand for marine tourist facilities).

The proposed Sicilian littoral plan, altough the only one of its kind, contains some methodological indications of great interest:
- the concept of the close integration of natural and cultural processes within the coastal areas;
- the particular nature of coastal planning being at the same time area planning (land and sea) and interface planning in relation to other forms of planning (sector and area) which leads inevitably to the adoption of comprehensive planning strategy.

However the awareness of the serious problems connected with negative developments on Italian littorals, demonstrated by numerous studies and pieces of research (one of them, the most systematic, has led to the pubblication of an "Atlas of Italian shores" which underlines all natural and cultural factors responsible for such development)(CNR, 1984) has led other regions (e.g. Calabria, Abruzzi, Molise, Emilia Romagna and Marche) to adopt intervention plans for all their coasts. Even when such plans were not limited at merely listing a series of conservation works to be carried out, they have not produced important results.

Such circumstances, together with a growing awareness of the damage and risks caused by pollution have brought about a significant transfer of focuses from the land to the sea.

An important step in this direction was made by the passing of act n. 979/1982 regarding regulations for the defence of the sea. The most important aim of this law is the drawing up by the Ministry of Mercantile Marine, in collaboration with the regions, of a general plan for defending the sea and the marine environment (2). The aim of this plan is to orientate, promote and coordinate intervention and activities regarding the conservation of the marine environment according to programming criteria and with particular emphasis on the forecasting of potentially dangerous events and the measures necessary to limit their effects and deal with them once they eventually happen (Min. Bilancio e Progr. Econ., 1985, 1986).

Among the most important aims there are:
- the organisation of a network for the observation of the quality of the marine environment permanently linked to operational centers and a suitable inspection system for activities carried out along the coast, for the fight against pollution, the administration of coastal areas and the conservation, including ecological conservation of marine resources;
- the absolute prohibition of the emission of harmful substance from ships in territorial waters, and for ships under the Italian flag even outside;
- the setting up of marine reserves which will include the sections of coast involved. All activities considered harmful may be prohibited in these reserves, including bathing and navigation (3).

This integration of coast and sea -the first recorded in Italy- goes even further because, when the marine reserve is adjacent to a national park or a national nature reserve, the coordination of administration of the two protected areas becomes obligatory in order to achieve a unified orientation.

The plan has not yet been implemented, but there has been intense activity on the part of the Council for the defense of the sea against pollution regarding the preparation of its guidelines. The most important points which have emerged are:
- the conception of the coast as a single reality made up of land and sea. Consequently, the need for efficient coordination of policies concerning the marine environment and that concerning coastal areas, bearing in mind that the latter is an inseparable component of a global policy on the sea and the coasts; in this respect act n. 979/1982 sets out an organisational framework for carrying out an integrated administration of the sea and the coastal areas;
- recognition of the fact that because of deteriorating environmental conditions it is not enough to set out to define compatibility of uses, but initiatives must be launched with the aim of environmental recovery. The most important steps to be taken by means of the plan are therefore protection and rehabilitation;
- emphasis upon the need for the programmed administration of State property along the coasts, since it is responsible for all forms of settlements in coastal areas and all uses of land for industrial and energy-producing purposes (4);
- the plan should apply to an area defined in a sufficiently unambiguous manner -the belt of demanio- and should be a master plan that can be implemented by means of projects. It is therefore necessary to define a general situation from which to derive priority operations; these

can be summarised as follows:
- regulations of the discarge of effluent into the sea;
- restoration of sedimentological balance (by intervening along the coasts and the hydrographic basins);
- definition of areas needing conservation;
- regulations of the use of marine State property;
- classification of beaches according to their carrying capacities;
- identification of channels for cooperation between central departments of State administration and local authorities.

Notes

1. The problem of the organisation of coastal areas forms partially the substance of the recent plan for tourist development prepared by the Puglia region, even if only from a "strategic" and sectorial point of view (Centro It. Studi Sup. Turismo and Regione Puglia, 1988).

2. Anti-pollution regulations include, on the landward side, acts n. 319/1976 and n. 650/1979 which control discharging of any kind, including that made directly into the sea; and act n. 915/1982, which controls waste disposal, including toxic and harmful substances.

3. Shortly before the passing of act n. 979/1982 the first two completely protected marine reserves in Italy, Ustica and Miramare, were created.

4. Marine State property ("demanio marittimo") occupies the belt adjacent to the sea including the shore and the beach. It has been administered with a mixed authoritarian and permissive approach and without any idea of protection or enhancement of the coastal areas. The reclamation of coastal State property should provide a strategic lever for reclamation work to be carried on further inland. It should not be forgotten that the State has exclusive control over territorial waters and the continental shelf.

REFERENCES

AA.VV.: Regioni: legge e decreto Galasso and dossier I Piani paesistici in Italia. Urbanistica Informazioni XIV, 18-25 and 56-80 (1986).
CENTRO ITALIANO DI STUDI SUPERIORI SUL TURISMO, REGIONE PUGLIA: Piano di Sviluppo Turistico. Fase di Analisi e Fase Propositiva. F.Angeli, Milano, 1988, 2 voll.
CNR: Atlante delle spiagge italiane. SELCA, Firenze, 1984.

14					COASTLINES OF ITALY

DOCTER - ISTITUTO DI STUDI E DOCUMENTAZIONE PER IL
	TERRITORIO: Annuario europeo dell'Ambiente 1986. Milano,
	1986.
ENEL: Atlante delle caratteristiche territoriali primarie
	delle coste italiane. Roma, 1973.
FIORELLI F.: Le variabili dell'organizzazione degli spazi
	costieri. In MURA P.M. (ed.), Una Geografia per la
	Pianificazione, 48-50. Gangemi, Reggio Calabria-Roma,
	1988.
GABRIELLI B.: Tecniche di pianificazione costiera. In MURA
	P.M.(ed.), Una Geografia per la Pianificazione, quot.,
	24-29, 1988
KARRER F.: La difesa delle coste nella pianificazione
	territoriale e urbanistica. Turismo Verde 5, 1, 7-10
	(1986).
KARRER F.: Pianificazione (o ri-pianificazione?) del
	territorio costiero nazionale. Porti Mare Territorio VI,
	3-4, 55-62 (1984).
LANDINI Pierg.; MURA P.M.: Riflessioni geografiche sul
	concetto di regionalizzazione nell'Urbanistica. Rivista
	Geografica Italiana LXXXIX, 273-302 (1982).
MINISTERO DEL BILANCIO E DELLA PROGRAMMAZIONE ECONOMICA:
	Progetto '80. Rapporto preliminare al Programma
	Economico Nazionale 1971-75. Roma, 1969.
MINISTERO DEL BILANCIO E DELLA PROGRAMMAZIONE ECONOMICA,
	ISTITUTO DI STUDI PER LA PROGRAMMAZIONE ECONOMICA:
	L'organizzazione territoriale delle fasce costiere
	italiane. Roma, 1974.
MINISTERO DELLA MARINA MERCANTILE, CONSULTA PER LA DIFESA
	DEL MARE DAGLI INQUINAMENTI: Relazione sulle Linee Guida
	per il Piano Generale di difesa del mare e delle coste
	dall'inquinamento e di tutela dell 'ambiente marino
	(Articoli 1, 3 e 26 della Legge 31 dicembre 1982,
	n.979). Roma, Jan. 1985.
MINISTERO DELLA MARINA MERCANTILE, CONSULTA PER LA DIFESA
	DEL MARE DAGLI INQUINAMENTI: Contributo (Questionario
	-Memorandum) alle iniziative delle regioni per il Piano
	Generale di difesa del mare e delle coste
	dall'inquinamento e di tutela dell' ambiente marino
	(Articoli 1, 3 e 26 della Legge 31 dicembre 1982,
	n.979). Roma, June 1986.
PINNA M. (ed.): Parchi nazionali e parchi regionali in
	Italia. Società Geografica Italiana, Roma, 1984.
PRANZINI E. (ed.): La gestione delle aree costiere.
	Edizioni delle Autonomie, Roma, 1985.
REGIONE EMILIA ROMAGNA, Assessorato Edilizia Urbanistica:
	Il Piano Paesistico Regionale. Bologna, June 1986.
REGIONE LIGURIA: Piano Territoriale di Coordinamento
	Paesistico. Documentazione di sintesi. Genova, 1986.
REGIONE LAZIO: Assessorato all'Urbanistica ed Assetto del
	Territorio, Assessorato alla Tutela Ambientale: Piani

territoriali   Paesistici.   Ambito   territoriale   n. 14
(Basso Lazio). Relazione. Roma, 1986.

REGIONE SICILIANA, Assessorato Territorio e Ambiente: Piano
Regionale per la difesa del litorale marino (L.R.
65/81).   Relazione   di   Piano,   Indicazioni   Azioni
Interventi (Draft Report 1^phase by Bonifica SpA). Roma,
Feb. 1988.

TOURING CLUB ITALIANO: Parchi e riserve naturali in Italia.
Milano, 1982.

UNITED NATIONS: Coastal Area Management and Development.
Department of International Economic and Social Affairs,
Ocean Economic and Technology Branch. Pergamon Press,
Oxford, 1982.

VALLEGA A.: La regione marittimo-litoranea: nuova categoria
di ricerca regionale. Rivista Geografica Italiana
LXXXVII, 4, 267-285 (1980).

VALLEGA A.: Towards the maritime coastal region. In
MUSCARA' C.; SORICILLO M.; VALLEGA A. (eds.): Changing
maritime transport, vol. II, 283-308. Istituto Univ.
Navale, Napoli, 1985.

VALLEGA A. : Organizzazione litoranea e gestione del mare.
In MURA P.M. (ed.), Una Geografia per la pianificazione,
quot., 12-23, 1988.

ZUNICA M.: Per un approccio all'interfaccia terra-mare.
Dipartimento di Geografia, Quaderno n. 5, Padova, 1986.

Influence of Rivers on Pollution of Coastal Waters

A. Bertoluzza, L. Boni, G. Bottura, G. Casalicchio, A. Chiesa,
M. Ciabatti, A.M. Felisa, E. Rabbi, A. Tinti, R. Viviani.*

Abstract

The pollution of fluvial and sea water by industrial activity, human settlement and agricultural practices, is a question of great topical interest and its study requires a research program involving many scientific fields. In this paper an interdisciplinary, methodological approach to the study of the influence of basin waters on the eutrophication of sea waters, along the Emilia-Romagna coasts, is outlined and the interaction of different "speciation" of continental and coastal environment is emphasized. The first results about the study of a sample basin, the Savio River, are reported.

Introduction

Our age is undoubtedly affected by the severe problem of waste disposal. This is the result of industrial activities, the urban settlement and the negative effects produced by some agricultural practices, such as fertilisation. It seems superfluous to remind here the different and well known examples of this situation, ranging from pollution of the surface and underground waters, to processes of eutrophication in sea waters. It seems important however to enhance the concept that such undesirable effects are mostly due to insufficient preliminary research, planned with the only aim to gather as many data as possible about the physical, chemical and biochemical processes that the human activities can start or modify.

To be useful and correct, such research programs require an interdisciplinary character and should involve different scientific fields such as chemistry, pedology, geology, hydrogeology, biology, environmental biotechnologies, biochemistry, etc..

---

* Centro di Ricerca Interdipartimentale delle Scienze del Mare (C.R.I.S.M.), Università degli Studi, via Zanolini 3, 40126 Bologna.

Moreover they should encompass a territorial framework as far wide as possible, because environmental damages occurring in a certain area are often originated in other regions and can have a sequence of causes and effects able to spread on long distances.

One of the clearest examples is that of a river basin whose waters interact with different pedotypes, crops, agricultural uses, pollutants before reaching the sea where they can locally alter the natural chemical, physical and biological conditions.

On these basis, this contribution is aimed to suggest a methodological model for the study of river waters influence on coastal pollution and particularly on the onset of algal blooms affecting the Emilia-Romagna coastal region.

Processes regulating exceptional sea-weeds development, and specifically the overgrowth of some species, are still scarcely known; each species or perhaps each subspecific entity, has different timing and growing conditions from the others; therefore it is rash to deduce data to advance generalized hypothesis.

Besides, the nutrient supply (phosphorus, nytrogen etc.) due to different human activities, to our opinion the humic substances, carried by rivers, could have great importance; consequently there is a need to study the catchment basin also in its geological, morphological and pedological aspects.

As far as the Adriatic Sea is concerned, eutrophic processes, even though they appeared in the past (the first reports date back to 1872 for the Gulf of Venice), have recently gained such proportions that bathing and fishing have been limited.

We choose the Savio river as sample basin (Fig.1), this being thought particularly suitable for its dimensions, anthropical activities (there are considerably large zootechnical activities), and finally for the high pollution of seawaters in the vicinities of its outlet.

The most important aspect of this research, from a methodological point of view, consists in the "speciation" of the examined area (continental and coastal environment) with the interaction of a wide range of disciplines. We refer to the term speciation as the proceedings and researches able to define the different phoenomena, from a quantitative and qualitative point of view, through a sistematical approach, enabling an outlook of their reciprocal relationships and correlations (Fig.2).

To reach this aim, the research usually requires:
a) Precise characterisations of the natural aspects of the basin such as: geological, morphological, pedological, hydrological, hydrogeological, vegetational and climatical features.

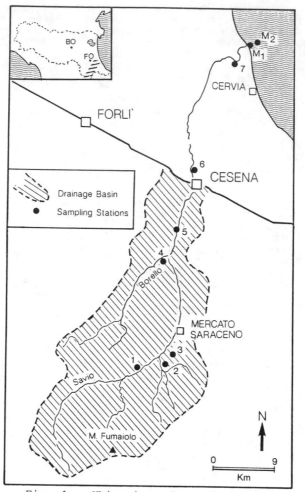

Fig. 1 — Ubication of sample basin

b) Analysis of the various human activities enhancing entity
and quality of the examined substances.

c) Analysis of the water and sediment features in the various
areas of sampling distributed along the river.

d) Analysis of sea waters and sediments near to the river
outlet and in the adjacent sea.

e) Production of thematical maps and a data base arrangement
of the different themes, allowing a comparative analysis.

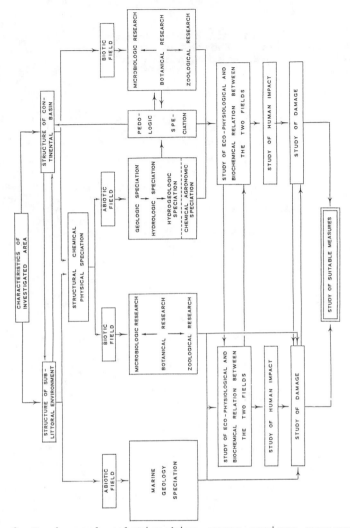

Fig. 2 — Reciprocal relationships among various researches

Methodology and preliminary results

Geological Speciation

It consists in a detailed survey aimed to individuate the lythological, structural, physical and mineralogical features of the pedogenetic substratum. The final product is a geolythological map at the scale of 1:10,000 or 1:5,000.

Hydrological Speciation

It aims to the evaluation of the water balance of the examined area, through the measure and estimation of its components (rains, surface, interflow and underground flow, and evapo-transpiration).

Hydrogeological Speciation

It tends to gather all necessary elements to know the depth, speed and direction of the underground flow, the water infiltration speed and their chemical features.

Pedological Speciation

It points out the distribution and characteristics of different pedological types. Soils and particularly A horizons are the most affected by the action of different pollutants running into the basin and more susceptible of interaction with them through mostly chemical processes. A large amount of elements and compounds can flow away towards the coast together with soils exposed to erosion.

The final results shown on a 1:25,000 scale are a pedological map and other maps concerning vegetation, cultivation practices, fertility etc.. It is necessary to compare and analyse them.

Marine-Geological Speciation

It aims to gather information about the nature, entity, spreading directions and behaviour in the sea of substances and compounds flowing into it from rivers; it requires data collecting about sea currents and chemical and physical features of seawaters and sediments.

Speciation of the Agricultural Environment

It consists in a characterisation of different agricultural activities and of the substances which are poured into the soil. Different kinds of farming, cattle breeding, and manufacturing of agricultural products operating in the basin are divided and gathered into different classes, and each class is marked by a "danger indicator" for the coastal and continental environment. This study also requires researches on the agronomical fertility, with particular regard to its chemical component.

Chemical, Physical and Structural Speciation

The study of chemical features in a part of the Savio river drainage basin and of their influence on the algal bloom on the northern part of the Adriatic Sea has been approached considering on one hand the chemical-physical parameters and on the other hand the profile of the speciation with the stability and instability of the marine echosystem and the dynamic of the process; these aspects do not yet have an adequate methodological approach.

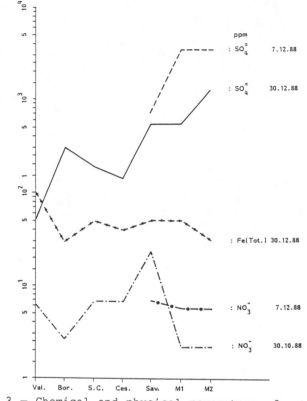

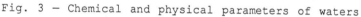

Fig. 3 — Chemical and physical parameters of waters

a) Chemical and physical parameters

Chemical and physical properties of fluvial and coastal waters in front of the outlet of the Savio river have been determined by four samplings gathered on 26th June, 28th July, 30th October, 7th December 1988.

Properties measured in situ are: pH, temperature, Eh, dissolved oxygen, electric conductivity; those measured in the laboratory: TH, TAC, cations (Ca, Mg, Na, K, total Fe and NH_4) and anions (SO_4, HCO_3, CO_3, NO_3).

These analyses, carried out on the Savio river and its affluents, aimed to define relationships existing between the chemism of fluvial waters on one hand, and the nature of the soil, industrial biocenosis and anthropic influence (urban and industrial settlements and intensive agriculture) on the other.

The studies performed along coast tend to find out the influence of rivers on sea waters, considering above all an

area in which the shore dynamic processes are conditioned by
artificial defense structures consisting in detached breakwaters, subparallel to the shoreline.

In both cases the researches will last not less than two
years, with seasonal terms and in coincidence with rainy
periods.

The results we obtained so far are represented on diagram
and gave the following information (Fig.3):

a1) Sulphate Content

The sampling gathered on October 30th enabled to ascer-
tain a more high level of the anion SO_4 in the Borello stream
(it is the main affluent of the Savio) in which outcrop
formations of the upper Miocene, with evaporites rich in
gypsum. Anion SO_4 decreases downstreams and then it increases again and this phoenomenon could be due to the salt-water
encroachement which is possible to observe at the Savio
outlet.

The samplings in the sea water on December 7th showed a
SO_4 concentration at the surface comparable to that of the
bottom, while under normal conditions this anion content
increases with depth so that a stratification settles and
prevents vertical movements of the water. Since copious rain
occurred ten days before the sampling and intense winds blew
for six days from W and SW, the likeliest hypothesis is that
the increased flow rates of the Savio and strong surface
marine currents, whose direction was from SW to NE, pushed
considerable water masses offshore and set a compensation
current that brought about an upwelling.

a2) Nitrate Content

NO_3 distribution (samples gathered on 30th October) shows
clear traces of the differences existing in the basin. As a
matter of fact, the lowest NO_3 concentrations are to be found
in areas where the zootechnical, urban and industrial settlements are modest or where agriculture is not exploited;
on the contrary, the highest NO_3 concentrations are above all
downstream the town of Cesena (80,000 inh.), where the conditions are reverse. NO_3 found in the seawater shows a considerable decrease in quantity.

During the upwelling and Savio greater flow rate, different NO_3 contents between continental and marine waters decrease considerably, with a slight increase in the first
case and a substantial decrease in the second one.

a3) Total Iron Content

The study of this element is particularly important because it is supposed, together with other organic compounds,
to contribute to the algal blooms. Iron is particularly
abundant in the highest basin areas, where the vegetation

consists mainly in conifers.

These conditions favour the iron mobilisation, given the presence of chelates and the low pH value in the soil. Iron decreases downstreams and keeps very low rates up to the river outlet.

b) Dimensional and Equilibrium Speciation

Four main speciations are to be taken into account: dimensional speciation; the speciation of the oxydizing state; of the equilibria; finally the kinetic speciation. Besides the traditional methods, adequate techniques such as: chromatographic techniques in the gaseous and liquid phase, isoelectrofocusing, infrared, nuclear magnetic resonance tecniques, molecular spectroscopic like Raman's vibrational techniques, etc., have been used to estimate the chemical–physical and structural factors and the characters of the marine echosystem, making also use of real condition simulating models and real systems.

Only methods concerning dimensional speciation and equilibrium speciation are discussed here.

Dimensional speciation (De Mora and Harrison, 1983) implies the study of the distribution of a certain "species" related to the particle dimensions; it was accomplished by dividing the samples (soil, sediment, fluvial and marine water estract etc.) into fractions, through filters with different molecular weights, according to the proceeding explained in (Fig. 4). Sructural measurements (vibrational

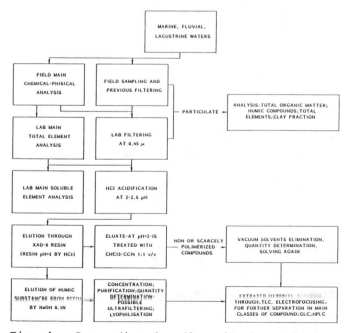

Fig. 4 — Proceeding for dimensional speciation

spectra etc.) were accomplished from the fractions characterized by different dimensions, and these point out the presence of molecular species showing different complexity
(e.g. in the inorganic field phosphates and polyphosphates);
while in the organic field low molecular weight species
like: amminoacids and more complex species such as humic
acids etc.. The problem of the separation and identification
of chemical species, able to influence the eutrophication
process and come from different situations, is important
because it allows the comparison and the evaluation of different contributions and the possible intervention to reduce
any kind of influence. The problem of humic acids (Russel et
al. Edit., 1983) draws our attention because literature data
and the tests we carried out demonstrate their influence on
the algal bloom phoenomenon (Aiken et al. Edit., 1985 and
Casalicchio, 1986).

The equilibrium speciation (Turner et al., 1981) was
achieved on the basis of the species concentration rates and
of the chemical-physical features of the water, of the equilibrium constants related to the possible different reactions between the tested species and the organic and inorganic matrixes. An estimate of the standard traditional methods became necessary, in order to point out their capabili-
ty to alter the equilibria existing among the species and to
find out more advanced methods not affecting these equilibria.

In order to confirm the preliminary tests indicating an
increase in the growth effect of the *Protogonyaulax tamarensis* when by phosphorus atoms parity, sodium metaphosphate
was added instead of sodic orthophosphate. It also turned to
be necessary to carry out prelyminary tests about the different forms of inorganic phosphorus. Equally important is the
spotting of the trasformation mechanisms regarding such
forms. These chemical physical and structural problems show
particular significance for the molecular definition of the
practicable equilibria within the echosystems influencing
particularly eutrophication.

Here the different inorganic phosphorus molecular species (ortho; di; tri.......metaphosphate) and their equilibria depending on pH, are characterized through laser Raman
vibration spectroscopy (Clark and Hester Edit., 1987).

Methaphosphate condensed forms in their linear or cyclic
structure contain anhydride links P-O-P, which can have hydrolysis reactions with the development of less complex species made, for activated complex, more reactive than the
species having a similar but not activated structure. The
demolition mechanism that the complex phosphorus species
e.g. polyphosphates endure over alcaline hydrolysis, was
simulated through the study of the demolition mechanism of
the polymeric chain caused by the nucleophil species ion-
oxygen.

Environmental and Microbiological Speciation

This aims to investigate how the microbic activities are able to influence the algal development and vice versa, making use of environmental and bacteriological researches carried out both on the basin soils and on coastal waters. The production of antibiotic substances by many algae, especially diatoms, is well known; on the other hand, many microbic species produce stimulating substances for the algal growth, while others are able to solubilize several forms of unsoluble phosphorate compounds etc.

Botanical Research

This kind of research, within the coastal environment, aims at the study of the planktonic, micro and macrobenthonic associations, of their distribution and periodicity and finally the growth factors of microalgae.

In the continental environment it tends to emphasize the distribution and periodicity of the fluvial planktonic and benthonic associations and to produce a map on real and potential vegetation. The researches carried out up to now in the coastal environment are focused on the analysis of humic substances and polyphosphate influence on the *Protogonyaulax tamarensis* growth.

The importance of the humic substances dissolved in marine water on the dinoflagellate has been studied for some time (Prakash et al., 1973). These substances derive mainly from the soil leaching caused by the rain to which it is possible to add a more or less important contribution (depending on the areas) due to phytoplankton and phytobenthos decomposition. The stimulus effect on the *P. tamarensis* growth was mainly observed for the low molecular weight fractions. Observations carried on the "red tides" that since 1975 (Boni 1983; Boni et al., 1986) have been originating almost every year in the NW part of the Adriatic Sea, show that they happen during summers when to a heavy rains period follows a period of high pressure and calm sea and great quantities of humic substances are poured into the sea, but not dispersed.

On the basis of bibliography and direct observation we decided to undertake a study dealing with the influence of these substances on the growth of dinoflagellates. We also decided to take into account the possibility that the algae use P sources different from orthophosphate, just adding poliphosphate to the growth soil.

The research was carried out using *Protogonyaulax tamarensis* as alga test. Even though this is not one of the most common species originating coloured tides in the Adriatic Sea, it is very interesting from a scientific point of view. It is widely known that within this species, there are toxine producing strain and other which are harmless. In 1985 the species isolated and clonated from Adriatic natural plankto-

nic association has been preserved in a Guillard and Ryther
f/2 and f/10 culture medium (Guillard and Ryther, 1962).
F/10, dilution 1:5 of f/2, contains also soil extract prepared with garden soil, but not treated with fertilizers or
herbicides. Both media were prepared by addition to natural
seawater, filtered at 0,45 μm, of macro and micronutrients.
The research, dealing with the humic substances influence on
P. tamarensis growth, was carried out by cultivating it with
appropriate f/2 and f/10 soils modifications:

f/2 prepared with seawater filtered through resins capable
of keeping every colloidal substance;
f/10 prepared with soil extract treated with the same resins
and in untreated seawater— f/10 prepared with soil extract
and seawater previously treated with resins;
f/2 in which the P source consists in poliphosphate;
f/2 and f/10 normal, used as control.

Every test was triplicated and the resulting growth rates
were studied for each culture, searching for the highest
cells number and the division number obtained during the
exponential growth period.

We observed that the cultures prepared with f/10 and
treated seawater and soil extracts did not show any algal
growth.On the contrary, biomass increases were found in other cultures and we report them following in an increasing
order:

f/10 prepared with normal soil and resins-treated water
f/10 normal
f/2 prepared with resins-treated water
f/2 treated whith polyphosphates
f/2 normal

Even though these are preliminary results and a basis for
future researches, we think that colloidal substances considerably influence the dinoflagellate growth; moreover that
they are able to use for their growth, sources different from
orthophosphate.

Zoological Research

This aims at studying the quality and quantity of plank-
ton, benthos and necton, as well as fluvial components.

Anthropic Activity Speciation

It is a very important integration of the previous researches because the knowledge of the quantity and quality
of industrial pollution sites in the basin becomes necessary, in order to estimate the entity of the substances dis-
charged into the ground, the waste disposal methods, the
location of the farms and the techniques of fertilisation.

Aimed Intervention Study

This interdisciplinar research has two main aims: on one hand the characterization of the different factors influencing in a direct or indirect way, the equilibrium of the system; on the other hand the planning of specific action in order to limit the negative effects of factors altering the normal situation in the considered areas. This second phase is as important as the first, and it involves advanced biotechnological treatments in the Savio drainage basin. In this way the effects of organic pollution brought about by cattle faeces, certainly can be reduced. On the other hand, diffused pollution sources such as fertilization, which usually involve a massive usage of chemicals, can be controlled and reduced by means of an adequate program of its use, and eventually adopting materials different from those deriving from synthetic processes.

Biotechnologies, in their actual development, will be able to support an aimed intervention both for biomolecular processes or techniques and proceedings referred to the different (urban, industrial, agricultural) components of the territory.

Coastal Eutrophication and Control of Dinoflagellate Toxins.

The toxins production of some algal species is a very important problem. As a matter of fact, the eutrophication process along the Emilia– Romagna coast has been occurring since 1975 with an excessive growth and reproduction of microscopic algae, particularly diatoms. Besides these microscopic seaweeds, macroscopic algae grow in such big quantities that they accumulate along the shore-line, and occupy the space between breakwaters and the shore, especially during summer.

When this phenomenon is accompanied by fishes, crustacea and other animals' mortality due to biotoxins, some dinoflagellata species are able to produce a phenomenon generally named "red tide".

Dinoflagellata known for their toxins production are: *Gonyaulax catenella, Gonyaulax tamarensis var. excavata, G. washingtoniensis, Exuviella mariae lebouriaem, Pyrodinium phoneus, Pyrodinium bahamensis, Cochlodinium sp.* and *Gymnodinium breve.*

Recent tests indicate the presence, for the same species, of non-toxic, toxic and intermediately toxic populations. On the contrary, no diatoms are thought to be toxin producers, and particularly *Skeletonema costatum,* either macroalgae *Ulva, Enteromorpha, Cladophora, Chaetomorpha, Enteromorpha* (green algae) or *Gracilaria* (red algae).
While the highest diatom blooms in the winter-spring period are characterized by one species only, *Skeletonema costatum,* the summer-autumn dinoflagellata "red tides" are characteri-

zed by other species, with a prevalence of *Gonyaulax polye-dra* and *Gymnodinium sp.*, similar to *Gymnodinium corii*. All the above quoted phenomena cause anoxia and the death of bivalve molluscs and other benthonic species. However, the main damage, especially as far as tourism is concerned, but also for coastal fishing, is represented by the "coloured tides".

The blooms of dinoflagellata that have been occurring on the Yugoslav coast since 1970 and on the coasts of Emilia-Romagna since 1975, focused the existence of a potential danger for this area as well, not only because the algal blooms are supported by species in the genera *Gonyaulax* and *Gymnodinium* (a group with many toxic species), but also because in 1982 a new species appeared similar to *Gonyaulax tamarensis*, a variety found in the Atlantic Ocean and in other seas, but never before in the Mediterranean. This species was linked with toxic shellfish in different zones of the world. This fact poses not only an ecological problem, but a health problem as well.

Since 1976 a monitoring to control the hydrosoluble (P.S.P. toxins, as saxitoxin and gonyautoxins) and fat-soluble toxins (N.S.P. toxins) biotoxins has been carrying out by the gathering of water samples, phytoplancton, bival-ve molluscs and fishes; particularly the following tests were performed:

1 Qualitative and quantitative analysis of the phytoplanc-ton.
2 Acute toxicity tests on fish using samples of water, phytoplancton extracts.
3 Acute toxicity tests on mice using samples of water, phytoplancton and mussel estracts for the determination of acid soluble toxins (PSP) *Gymnodinium breve* toxins and other fat-soluble toxins.
4 Chemical determination of saxitoxin based on the fluore-scence characteristics of an oxidation product of saxito-xin.

Using these techniques, it was possible to demonstrate the absence of biotoxins with acute ichytoxic effects as well as the absence of a neurotoxin affecting man during the "green tide" produced by *Gymnodinium sp.* similar to *Gymnodi-nium corii*, and the red tide of *Gonyaulax polyedra* and *Proto-gonyaulax tamarensis* sensu Fukujo. Water with blooms of *Pro-rocentrum micans* has also been shown to be nontoxic.

The researches are now being conducted using chromato-graphic methods (such as TLC and HPLC) for the separation of the various components of acid soluble fraction of a toxic *Gonyaulax tamarensis* (of the Atlantic coast of the United States) and comparing this with the nontoxic Adriatic *Proto-gonyaulax tamarensis*. In order to comprehend the biochemical mechanisms at the basis of the dinoflagellate monospecific blooms *P. tamarensis*, *G. polyedra* and *Gymnodinium sp.* and of their toxinology, it is very important to study the Savio basin and its nutrients' contribution to the coastal area where the phenomenon of anthropogenic eutrophication occurs. As a matter of fact, recent studies show that macronutrients, micronutrients and stimulating substances support the development of a single dinoflagellata; also that phosphorus, orthophosphates and nitrates are able to influence saxitoxin and gonyautoxins biosynthesis.

Acknowledgement

We thank P. Ferrieri And E. Prata for the considerable help in field and laboratory research

References

Aiken, G.R.; McKnight, D.M. (Ed.): Humic substances in soil, sediment and water. John Wiley & Sons 1985

Boni, L.: Red tides of the coast of Emilia-Romagna (northwestern Adriatic Sea) from 1975 to 1982. Inf. Bot. Ital., 15, 18-24 (1983)

Boni, L.; Pompei, M.; Reti, M.: Maree colorate e fioriture algali lungo le coste dell'Emilia-Romagna dal 1982 al 1985 con particolare riguardo alla comparsa di *Protogonyaulax tamarensis*. Nova Thalassia, 8, 237-245 (1986)

Casalicchio, G.: Il fosforo, l'agricoltura, l'ambiente. Esercitaz. Accadem. Agraria, 3, 18, 147-276, Pesaro 1986

Christian, R.F.; Gjessing, E.T.: Aquatic and terrestrial humic materials. Arbour Science Publ. 1983

Clark, R.J.H.; Hester, R.E.: Spectroscopy of inorganic-based materials. Advances in Spectroscopy, 14. John Wiley & Son 1987

De Mora, S.J.; Harrison, R.M.: The use of physical separation techniques in trace metal speciation studies. Water Res., 17, 723 (1983)

Guillard, R.R.L.; Ryther, J.H.: Studies on marine planktonic diatoms 1st *Cyclotella nana* Husted and Detanula convervacea (Cleve). Gran. Can. J. Microbiol., 8, 229-239 (1962)

Prakash, A.; Rashid, H.A.; Jensen, A.; Subba Rao, D.V.: Influence of humic substances on the growth of marine phytoplankton: diatoms. Limnol. Oceanogr., 18(4), 516524 (1973)

Turner, D.R.; Whitfield, M.; Dickson, A.G.: The equilibrium speciation of dissolved components in fresh water and sea water at 25°C and 1 atm pressure. Geochim. Cosmochim. Acta 45, 855 (1981)

EUTROPHICATION IN THE ADRIATIC SEA

Corrado Piccinetti* and Giovanni Bombace**

Abstract

The different situations called "eutrophication" in the Adriatic sea have been considered. The general situation of the Adriatic, the biological characteristics of phytoplankton population have been exposed in order to explain the different phenomena. The increased number of red tide will be explained by the high quantity of wash water decharged by disposal plant.

During these last few years, owing to the phenomena of the abnormal multiplication of some species of marine algae (seaweeds) and to the troublesome consequences which arose from it, above all for summer tourism, great attention has been paid to these facts, both from tourist operators and from bathers; as well as from the press and the mass media in general.

Alarming and dramatic news spread eround and great confusion, was generated on the causes of the phenomena, along with possible remedies to be adopted.

The word "eutrophication" has been emphasized in catastrophic terms and the press spoke about "The dying Adriatic sea": it isn't know from where they received this news.

This short report aims at clarifing some aspects of the phenomenon, to point out the black spots of it to develop some reflections which may be of help for those who must take decisions about it.

We consider it useful, however, in order to understand the phenomenon, to give a short description of the ecologi-

---

*   Laboratorio di Biologia Marina e Pesca - Viale Adriatico, 52 - 61032 FANO (ITALY)
** Istituto Ricerche Pesca Marittima - Molo Mandracchio - 60100 ANCONA (ITALY)

cal aspect of the Northern and Central Adriatic, which are the basins structurely interested in the phenomenon of the blooms.

The Adriatic sea has a surface of 138.000 Kmq, equal to 1/20 of the whole Mediterranean. Its water volume is of 35.000 Kmc, equal to 1/125 of the same. Nevertheless the Nothern and Central Adriatic receive a huge quantity of continental water mainly coming from rivers on the Italian coast, from the Isonzo to the Fortore. The medium total flow of this group of rivers is 3.097 mc/s. Of it, 51 % equal to a water flow of 1.580 mc/s belongs to the Po, 34 % equal to 1.061 mc/s belongs to the rivers which flow out to the North of the Po, starting from the Isonzo and just 15 % equal to 455 mc/s belongs to the rivers South of the Po, from the Reno to the Fortore.

It is remarkable quantity of fresh water, especially of the Po, which causes, conditions of great fertility and riches for fisheries. Following persistent rains, this water flow may result much more abundant causing unexpected and high supply of nutrients (nitrates and phosphates). To the North-West of the Adriatic basin the salinity range is lower than 30 %. . On the surface, owing to continental water flows, in many points of the Veneta and Emiliano-Romagnola marine belt the salinity is lower than 25 %. (Franco, 1985).

Off-shore and eastward along the Yugoslavian coast, the salinity is higher than 38-38,5 %. especially at deeper water, where the influence of the "Oriental waters" is felt.

The difference of salinity, and therefore of the density, in the extreme thermic seasons, favours the circulation or "gradient currents" flowing into the Mediterranean waters, through the channel of Otranto.

Also fromthe point of view of the water temperature, the Adriatic is quite differentiated, with thermic seasonal differences above 20°C.

In summers, in the Northern Adriatic there may be maximum temperatures around 28°C, in winter there is a very low temperature down to about 5°C, especially when the cold and dry "bora" winds blow, causing intense evaporation.

In this way dense and cold waters are formed, sinking and touching the bottom, running southward, giving origin to the deep waters which fill the middle Adriatic trench and crossing the straits of Otranto, to the Ionian Sea.

These thermic events determine ecological and biological phenomena of remarkable importance, especially in the Central and Northern Adriatic. In winter when the surface temperature decreases, there is a thermic inversion, therefore the deep layers off-shore, show a higher temperature than those near to the coast. This causes a great horizontal migration of species, from the coast to the open sea (red-

mullets, gurnards, cuttle-fish), from the beginning of the
autumn.

In winter a vertical barrier of dense water forms, which
divides the less dense coastal waters from those off-shore.
This barrier keeps, practically entangled in a nearly closed "basin", the nutrients (nitrates and phosphates) which
come from the water flows and mainly from the Po.

In spring when this front begins to flake, there is more
light and the temperature rises; the phytoplankton has
abundant food, and consequently the zooplankton (that is
the herbivorous species) and all other links of the feeding
chain up to fishes.

In summer instead, if the sea is calm, around the coast
is formed a horizontal barrier which discriminates water
layers of different density. Surface waters enriched with
continental waters mix with them and for the absence of
winds, the convective re-mixing movements of water layers
are lacking; the bottom waters may be lacking in oxygen;
the water temperature is elevated and doesn't favour the
dissolution of oxygen itself. This is an ideal situation
for the beginning of the algae bloom phenomenon.

These characteristics essentially concern the high and
middle Adriatic basins, ecologically more analogous in comparison with the low Adriatic.

Among nutrients, phosphorus and nitrogen, are those
which determine the productive capacities of a water body.
Without entering into the matter of "the inhibiting factor"
on problems of relationship between nitrogen and phosphorus
in an equilibrated water body etc., it must be remembered
that, on the basis of the quantity of phosphorus/orto-
phosphate (P/PO_4) or of the total phosphorus (P tot.) it
is possible to distinguish different levels of sea water
throphication, according to the following table:

P/PO_4	WATERS	P TOTAL
2 - 5 µg/l	oligothrophics	below 10 µg/l
5 - 10 µg/l	mesotrophics	10 - 20 µg/l
10 - 20 µg/l	eutrophics	20 - 40 µg/l
above 20 µg/l	ipertrophics	above 40 µg/l

From research developed in the last ten years by Italian
and Yugoslavian authors, elaborating the data of the different stations of the high and middle Adriatic, according
to middle-seasonal values for several years, it has been
found that up to 4 - 5 miles from the coast, to the North
of the Po outlet (east of Chioggia), on the basis of
phosphorus and ortophosphate, one can find conditions of
eutrophic levels, more remarkable in winter than in summer.

With the exception of a radial distance about ten miles

around the Po mouths, area of eutrophication, the situation of the Northern Adriatic coastal waters varies between conditions of structural oligotrophy and temporary mesotrophy. The situation of the Southern Adriatic coasts mainly shows conditions of oligotrophy. From these eutrophic areas spreads an energy which, through food chains and then through biologic mediators, is transferred to fishing resources, both along coast and off-shore.

As a proof of the relationship existing among eutrophication, biological productivity and fishing, some data of fisheries and some statistic elaboration are useful.

Considering the contribution to the national fish catches of different Italian seas and calculating the average of the catches in the years 1982-1986, the Adriatic contributes to more than 50 %. Within the Adriatic, 48 % of the catch comes from the Northern and Middle part, and about 22 % is due to catches of the Emilia-Romagna coast, that is to the region with the highest level of eutrophication (Bombace, 1985).

If a more accurate calculation is made one can realize that one unit of fishing effort (i.e. n. 1 horse-power) produces in the high Adriatic about 600 Kgs of catch, in the middle Adriatic about 580 Kgs, while in other seas the values vary from about 100 to about 500 Kgs.

Over a number of years attention has been centred upon limiting factors, namely on nutrients and particularly on phosphorus, considered one of the principal cause of algal blooms, and upon the consequences to tourism and fishing. However this is not so. Eutrophication, that is the increase of nitrates, phosphates and of organic particulate matter, is believed to be the base of the productivity in the sea; and that this process induces the phytoplanktonic and phytobenthic organisms to organic mineral salts and grow. On the other hand, owing to the distance from the coast or from the sources of nutrients, the content of nitrates and phosphates is to some extent constant and the quantities rise in relation to events connected to the flow of the rivers. The excess of nutrients are absorbed by sediments, which in primary conditions release the nutrients in the same water.

If phosphates and the phosphorus were directly responsabile for the blooming, it would follow that algal blooms would occur in the Adriatic almost daily, because there is always in nearshore waters, a quantity of nutrients, sufficient to sustain a bloom. Observations and studies have led to a different conclusion, as blooms may only occur in particular meteomarine and oceanoqraphic conditions. These conditions are that of a calm sea (and therefore stratified), an elevated temperature, intense luminosity, without wind and contributions of fresh water.

All these characteristics may be found in the Adriatic and cause a situation of blooming. Obviously blooms occur at the expense of nutrients, therefore it may be said that nitrates and phosphates constitute necessary but not sufficient factors.

In the course of the last ten years, blooms of dinoflagellata (red tides) have resulted more frequent in the Adriatic, as has the situation of anoxia (deficiency of oxygen) in the bottom waters (Piccinetti and Manfrin, 1969).

In the course of one year, bloomings between April and November may be sustained by different species that occur in these months, with the characteristic that the bloom is identical in the same period also for distant areas.

For example, in spring and summer blooms are sustained by species of the Gonyaulax, Prorocentrum, Peridinium, Ceratium, Noctiluca genus, while in autumn they are based on species belonging to the Gymnodinium genus (Boni, 1985). These monospeciphic blooms of the Dinoflagellata are the ones which cause the most serious effects on the environment and resources, with consequences on tourism and fishing. A "Red tide" dispenses in whatever phase of development of the blooming process when a heavy sea storm intervenes and breaks the stratification and stirs up the waters.

Blooms sustained by Dinoflagellata, normally a minority group in the phytoplankton, dont seem connected to the contributions of phosphorous and azote (nitrogen) salts, but to a complex of causes, some of which are natural and others related with man's activities.

A natural cause, as we have seen, is the vertical stratification of water due to particular meteomarine conditions (calm seas for some days), which favours selectively the Dinoflagellata on the Diatomea. The anthropic factor is related to the heavy touristic concentration and the waters of the waste disposal plants which are discharge at a short distance from the shore. Beside salts (nitrates and phosphates) readily usable by surface phytoplankton these waste waters contain, substances that stimulate growth (biostimulants) and particularly vitamin B12, which can actively increase the process and the rate of multiplication of the Dinoflagellata.

It should be reminded that disposal plants receive waste in the order of tens of thousands of cubic metres of water a day. For example, along the coast of Emilia-Romagna these plants pour into the sea, near the shore, around a million cubic metres of water a day. Lastly, this enormous quantity of fresh water that flows into the sea further encourages density stratification of coastal waters.

This action could explain why, for example 50 years ago, we could suppose that a month of a calm and stratificated sea would have been needed to make the Dinoflagellata reach the critical concentration, whereas today ten days can be enough. Because the conditions of stratification for a period of ten days are certainly more frequent than that of one month, this explains the greater frequency of blooming and of anoxy by Dinoflagellata.

As regards the oxygen crises on the sea bottom (anoxy, ipoxy), they are related to a series of concurrent factors and may take place even without the blooms of the algae. The final result of the oxygen crisis is the death of the organisms tied to the sea bottom or those that have little mobility and the escape of the mobile organisms from the area concerned.

Anoxy establishes gradually and finds support in the following factors: elevated temperature, water of the lower salinity in surface, stability of the water flow with reduced mixing and diffusion of the oxygen, large biomasses on the bottom that use high quantities of oxygen for respiration connected to intense metabolism (warm waters); contribution of organical substances from the soil that consume oxygen for the process of oxidization. It is easily understood how such situation, with the negative balance of oxygen, comes to a progressive reduction of oxygen, until creating a situation not compatible with life, of organisms sensible to an oxygen deficiency and then of all the others involved in the putrefactive processes of the previously dead organisms.

When a strong sea storm arrives, it breaks the stratification and carries oxygen to the bottom, starting the recolonization process.

In 1977 this particular form of anoxy took place, unconnected to the development of the vegetal component, in a vast area of the high Adriatic, stretching from the Italian coast to the Yugoslavian waters with the death of the organisms of the bottom and the escape of the fish from the anoxic area.

The bloomings that happened in the month of August 1988 had started in June-July; they were due to benthic Diatomea Pennatae of the Navicula genus and have extended to a large area, also to the fact that the mucilaginous material was carried by the sea currents and therefore also beyond the area where the blooms firstly happened. This material is not only unpleasant for bathing, harmful even if it doesn't harm people, but it is also harmful to fishing activity, as it makes nets heavy, obstructs the meshes and causes loss of time for their cleaning.

The first description of a phenomenon of similar magnitude, came about in August 1872, and was made by Castracane, for the area of Fano and by Syrski for the Gulf of Trieste (Zanon, 1931).

It is a heavy mistake to consider that the Adriatic is

an equal and homogeneous basin. The Adriatic is a complex system, articulated and diversified in function of the latitude, of different physico-chemical and biological parametres and in function the distance from the coast. Therefore the Adriatic can be divided into the high, the middle and the low Adriatic (the first two more alike), a coastal under-system and one off-shore, a Yugoslavian coastal Adriatic and an Italian one completely different. Also there is a winter-spring Adriatic and a summer-autumn Adriatic, which are extremely different. To speak therefore of the Adriatic in wide sense means generalizing something that it is not.

As to fisheries, the Adriatic is the richest basin among the different seas which surround Italy.

The high and middle Adriatic are the richest in absolute. That certainly is due to the energetic input and therefore to the process of eutrophication, which is largely positive for resources and fishing. The Adriatic is therefore a sea which is very far from dying, even if the resources must be better managed.

As to the bloomings one must distinguish those from macroalgae (<u>Ulva</u>, <u>Enteromorpha</u>, <u>Gracilaria</u>) which obstruct sometimes wharfs and cliffs; the seasonal blooms of the Diatomea bound to fresh water contributes and to the flood conditions (spring, autumn, winter) and which, generally, haven't caused in the Adriatic negative environmente effects, with the death of fish; the "historical" blooms of Benthonic Diatomea with great production of mucilages (dirty sea of the authors of the 1800's) which obstruct the nets, of which the last is the one that happened during this year and lastly those of the Dinoflagellata (red tide) frequent in these last ten years and which seem bound to certain anthropic events (mass tourism, fall out of the depurators etc.).

These three groups of factors act in developing the blooms:
a) particular meteomarine and oceanographic conditions (calm sea, high temperature, stratification of the water mass, fresh water apports); it is a indispensable condition for blooms;
b) presence of nutrients (nitrates and phosphates); this is a necessary condition but not sufficient;
c) anthropic factors which increase near the coast, the presence of nutrients, disposal plants, artificial reefs, structures and basins with scarce water replacement, etc.

The consequences of blooms and anoxia, with economical damages for tourism and fishing and with negative environmental effects, call for remedies and solutions.

The complexity of the processes described in this report show, how hard it is and sometimes useless and enormously expensive propose therapies and solutions which do not consider the facts.

Strategies aiming to intervene on factors of point b) it mean to deceive to solve the problem of blooms.

On the other hand, in order to obstruct or to reduce blooms, the subtraction of nutrients should be of such an entity that the Adriatic would risk becoming a poor sea, not forgetting that the coastal marine sediments are impregnated with nutrients (nitrates and phosphates) which are left in the water.

It must be said, just to be clear, that the repairing of rivers and of the water-bearing stratum because of the various poisons which are poured into and because of particularly dangerous chemical substances, from the heavy metals and from the pesticides it is a truth on which everybody agrees, but has nothing to do with blooms.

Therefore the group of anthropic factors mentioned in point c) remains the only one on which man can reasonably interfere to eliminate or reduce a certain kind of blooms (Piccinetti, 1985).

Interventions aiming to pour off-shore with suitable pipes the cloacal liquids, would fertilize the waters off-shore which are poor of nutrients and provide a better protection for coastal waters.

Among other things submarine pipes suitably reinforced, might form "artificial reefs" suitable for the repeoplement of fauna and potential obstacles to illegal trawling.

As an alternative disposal waters might be used in agriculture. Lastly we must remember that a strategy of recycling of nutrients in the sea is possible, besides agriculture by means of enterprise on a large scale of marine culture and for a multi-purpose artificial reefs. Of course, an integration of the various solutions and value of the importance of the energetic systems (biological, technological, economic etc.) which are involved, should always be found out.

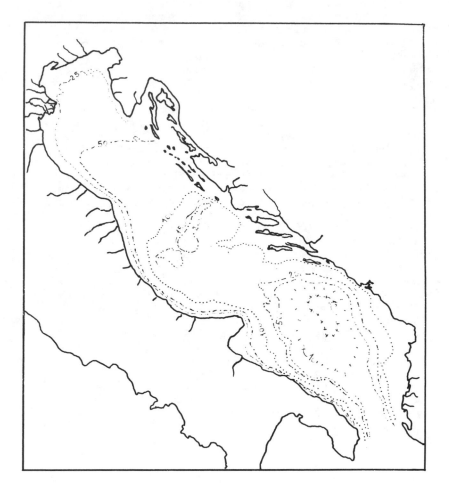

0 ———— 100 km

Fig. 1 – Bathymetry of the Adriatic sea (depth
        in metres).

REFERENCES

Bombace, G.: Eutrofizzazione, pesca e zone protette. Atti
    Conv. Naz. "Eutrofizzazione. Quali interventi?", Ancona
    novembre 1985.
Boni, L.: Problematiche del fitoplancton in Adriatico. Atti
    Conv. Naz. "Eutrofizzazione. Quali interventi?", Ancona
    novembre 1985.
Castracane degli Antelminelli, F.: Sulle faldoline che co-
    privano ovunque il mare Adriatico. Mem. Pont. Acc. Nuovi
    Lincei, Vol. XXV, Roma 1872.
Franco, P.: Caratteristiche oceanografiche dell'Adriatico
    settentrionale. Atti Conv. Naz. "Eutrofizzazione. Quali
    interventi?", Ancona novembre 1985.
Piccinetti, C.: Ipotesi di interventi sull'eutrofizzazione.
    Atti Conv. Naz. "Eutrofizzazione. Quali interventi?",
    Ancona novembre 1985.
Piccinetti, C.; Manfrin, G.: Osservazioni sulla mortalità
    di pesci e di altri organismi verificatasi nel 1969 in
    Adriatico. Note Lab. Biol. Mar. e Pesca, Fano, Vol. III
    (4), 1969.
Syrski, D.: Sulle masse glutinose osservate nei mesi di Giu-
    gno e Luglio 1872 nella parte settentrionale dell'Adria-
    tico. Relazione prodotta all'I.R. Governo Marittimo di
    Trieste. Tip. Hermanstofer, Trieste, 1872.
Zanon, V.: Esame di un campione di "mare sporco" del golfo
    di Fiume. Mem. Pont. Acc. Nuovi Lincei, Serie II, Vol.
    XV, 1931.

Coastal Pollution in Italy

Silvino Salgaro*

Summary

The pollution of the sea derives, like the greater part of those situations of environmental deterioration, from human activities. Industry, agriculture, leisure, settlements along the coast and also in the hinterland, combine to produce pollutant substances which sooner or later, directly or indirectly, reach the sea. Not for nothing is the sea water first vapour in the atmosphere and fresh water in the lakes and rivers. The complexity of the problem requires an interdisciplinary approach which examines the entire complex of human activities and the environment as a whole and which goes beyond national boundaries not only for a greater knowledge and protection of resources, but also for a better quality of life today and above all, tomorrow.

Introduction

Pollution of coastal waters began to show itself in Italy gradually, along with the development of an industrial society. Economic affluence and mass consumption did result in environmental changes, the intensity and frequency of which alarmed the government to the degree that, from about 1970, the first legal sanctions were issued on the protection of waters.

At first these regulations seem often disconnected from a comprehensive approach to the problem. In fact we pass from the law concerning the biodegradability of synthetic detergents (law March 3rd, 1971, no. 125) to the control of refuse dumping in maritime waters (law April 16th, 1976, no. 126) up to the law which provvided for regulations against water pollution, (May 10th, 1976 no. 319). But it is only with the law of August 28th 1980, no. 662, which occurred with the ratification of the international convention for the "prevention of pollution by ships" that Italy conformed to the EEC recommendation on

----

*Professor at the University of Verona, Faculty of Magistero, Institute of Geography, 37129 Verona.

the protection of water conditions. (Greco 1985)

Notwithstanding these measures and some regional laws (most of which issued around 1980), pollution has been a matter of consideration, mostly in local news, calling not only for research and speedy action but also for initiatives on part of environmentalist associations.

The most exact and detailed data concerning water conditions are supplied by local health authorities which carry out analyses of the water over the whole national territory for the Ministry of Health. These are supported by research carried out by groups in collaboration with specialised agencies.

Data published by the Ministry of Health refer to the conditions of bathing waters (Ministry of Health 1987). Analysis of samples started in 1984 in response to EEC Directive no. 160 of 1976, prescribing two samples for month for the period between April 1st. and October 1st. along the entire Italian coast, with a spatial frequency of 2 kms. According to that directive the safety levels for bathing in coastal waters were defined through 10 parameters of microbiological life (general coliforms, faecal coliforms and streptococcus) chemical and physical factors, (Ph, colour, transparency, presence of oils, phenols, surface active agents and oxygen). Whereas the first have a direct connection with the health of humans and serve to indicate the level of faecal pollution plus other and more dangerous factors such as some viruses, the latter tend to show unfavourable environmental conditions from an aesthetic point of view but favourable to the rise of degrading processes such as eutrophication.

The law envisages the possibility of beeing exempted by measuring same parameters of the latter group in all Regions. This applied to Sardinia for the quantification of oxygen in solution, and to Veneto, Emilia-Romagna, Marche, Tuscany and Lazio for the reduction of transparency limits.

Further initiatives have been launched in the meantime. Among these the most significant seem to be that of the "Lega-Ambiente" Association and of the "Kronos 1991" environmentalist Association.

The studies, carried by the ship Goletta Verde now represent a standard feature of the summer season (Lega Ambiente 1987). The campaign conducted in 1988, following those in 1986 and 1987, has carried out around 500 samplings and conducted about 900 chemical and bacteriological analyses along the entire Italian coastline. Beside the analyses related to the parameters on the safety levels of bathing waters, the research carried out by the Lega Ambiente was addressed for the first time to the isolation of the most common agricultural pesticides (twelve) and to several heavy metals, amongst which are chrome (Cr 6+) lead, mercury and arsenic.

The studies conducted by the "Kronos 1991" Association, instead had the purpose to test if the water on some popular beaches was suitable for swimming.

The sampling, carried out on the same day and time at every location by means of a standard procedure and with identical equipment and instruments, was done a few metres from the seashore and at an approximate depth of one metre. The analyses were completed within 24 hours, taking into consideration 30 different parameters to identify also the degree and origin of possible types of pollution not included by the regulations as not having an influence an higienical conditions. The study, repeated at varying times during the summer, has shown up situations and aspects which are often contradictory.

Spatial distribution of pollution

Conditions of the Italian seas seem rather precarious[1] everywhere, even if the degree and types of pollutants vary in relation to the causes which produce it and to measures taken to control its effects.

The Adriatic sea seems to be the most polluted particularly in the north central sector because of more shallow waters and slow water exchange. The situation is better in the other seas which are deeper and have stronger currents.

At a local level the situation becomes more homogeneous in so much as the pollution along the coast does not present great differences from Region to Region. Greater differences instead are noted in the type of pollutants and, to some degree, in the temporal distribution of the amounts of pollution. (Fig. 1)

Along the coasts it is possible to further identify a relative scale of critical points on which the phenomena prove to be most marked. The areas where the highest pollution levels are found are at the mouths of rivers, corresponding to urban areas and near to industrial discharges.

Among heavy metals, lead is spread along almost the whole coast. For this reason it seems that its presence should be imputed to the high level of vehicles circulating. Emitted into the atmosphere by motor exhausts, lead is deposited on the land and through the washing effects of rain, it ends up in the rivers and subsequently in the seas. It is also used in the metal industry and for this reason the concentration from such production units is highest in the areas of discharge (Liguria, Campania, Calabria, Basilicata, Puglia, Marche and Veneto) where major installations are located near the coast.

Mercury, much used in industry usually as a catalyst in various production processes and particularly in the pharmaceutical industry, is reported along the coasts of Tuscany, Liguria, Marche, Abruzzo and Veneto.(AA. VV. 1988)

In quantities below the level regarded as dangerous appear chrome (Liguria, Tuscany, Lazio, Campania and Calabria) arsenic (Tuscany, Campania, Calabria, Abruzzo).

Among other heavy metals, traces of copper, zinc nickel, cadmium and cobalt have been noted[2].

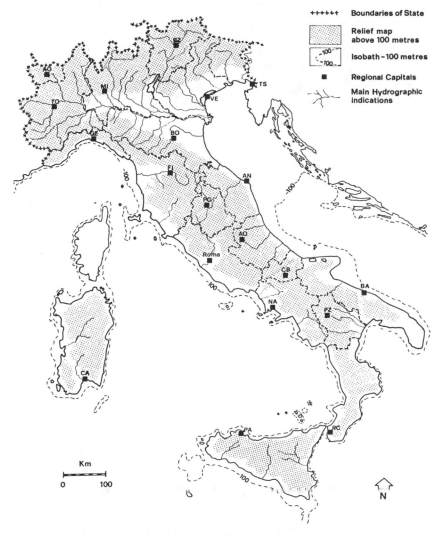

Fig. 1 - Morphological features of Italy.

However the most dangerous and widespread pollution of industrial origin [3] is that caused by phenols and mineral oils. Widely used in the plastics colourings, detergents and pharmaceutical industries, the phenol group based on a carcinogenic molecule is reported along coastal stretches where chemical industry is most widespread. Changes in the water owing to the mineral oils turn out to be expecially evident near commercial ports, and also tourist resorts and petrochemical industries.

Chemicals and pesticides used in agriculture also represent a serious cause of water pollution. (Fig. 2)

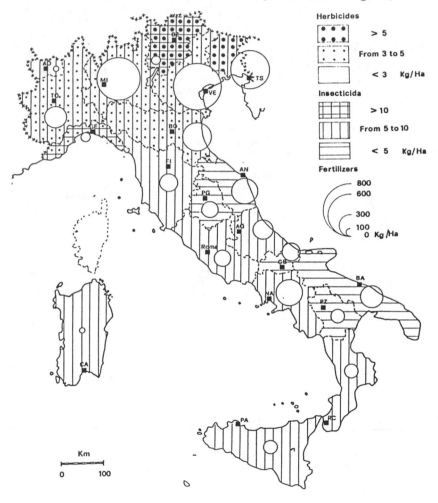

Fig. 2 —   Chemicals uses in agriculture (kg per hectare of cultivated land).

Particularly significant concentrations were noted
along the Ligurian coast and those of Tuscany, Lazio,
Campania and Veneto. The so called "riviera of flowers" in
Liguria presents rather high percentages of insecticides,
fungicides and fertilisers due to the intensive cultivation
of flowers carried out on the terracings at the back of the
shore. We find huge quantities of chemicals end up in all
the above mentioned Regions, even if along the coasts of
the Tyrrhenian Sea and above all, the Adriatic, besides the
usual presence of pesticides, other substances,
specifically used in certain crops are noted in
considerable percentages, examples of this are lindane,
used for the disinfection of soil, or bentazone, molinate
and athrazine, employed to eradicate grass in fields where
maize and other cereals are grown.

Also originating from agriculture and intensive
breedings[4] are the considerable amounts of nitrogen and
phosporus which contribute to the spread of eutrophication
in the Adriatic[5].

This process is also encouraged by large amounts of
urban wastes.

Biological pollution due to urban and industrial
wastes causes another type of highly dangerous water
deterioration, especially when different elements come into
contact and combine into new substances (Berbenni-Galassi,
1978). Changes produced by solid wastes derived from mining
and the processing of materials extracted from quarries
represent another danger for the quality of the water,
equal to the pollution caused by thermo-electric and
nuclear plants, which raise the temperature of the water
(Fig. 3) thus altering biological processes in the aquatic
flora and fauna (Martinis, 1987).

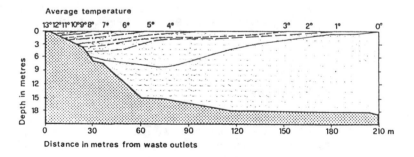

Fig. 3 -   Isotherm rates influenced by hot water discarges
            from a nuclear power station.

Microbiological pollution, constituted by non-
pathogenic coliforms and streptococchus, is distributed in

varying percentages along the entire coastline, accentuated
in vicinities of large urban areasand at the mouths of
rivers, and it yields values somewhat differentiated in
relation to the presence of waste disposal plants.

As a whole, the situation appears very complex (Tab.1)
In the vicinities of large urban areas, we find situations
in which the waste disposals function only partially
because they are too small or because they are still
incomplete, or not connected rationally and completely to
the sewage system. (Bari, Trani, Firenze etc.).

Region	Coastal length km.	Number of survey sites	Number of samples	Number of samples per site	Positive samples
Friuli V. G.	93,5	46	592	12,9	77,1%
Veneto	141,2	82	965	11,8	93,3%
Emilia R.	112,0	75	814	10,9	96,3%
Marche	166,0	212	2.485	11,7	88,2%
Abruzzo	134,0	135	1.522	11,3	68,5%
Molise	35,0	33	396	12,0	97,7%
Puglia	870,0	425	4.545	10,7	96,6%
Basilicata	65,7	43	461	10,7	81,9%
Calabria	487,8	545	3.694	6,8	71,7%
Campania	502,0	352	4.214	12,0	74,1%
Lazio	340,0	177	1.776	10,0	89,4%
Tuscany	527,9	296	3.650	12,3	89,4%
Liguria	316,6	306	3.758	12,3	91,2%
Sicily	1.244,5	551	3.792	6,9	78,3%
Sardinia	1.849,0	523	5.416	10,4	97,5%
Italy	7.052,0	3.801	38.070	10,0	86,0%

Tab. 1 -   Results following research on the quality of
            bathing waters - 1988 (Ministry of Health DPR
            470/82)

It follows that microbiological pollution tends to
have a spatial distribution predominantly irregular, which
can show opposite cases in the same region (Sicily includes
the province of Catania with 100% of positive samples, as
compared whit Caltanisetta with 60% negative results). In
fact many coastal towns on the Adriatic and Tyrrhenian
riviera where tourism is an important part of the local
economy, show a completely positive situation, especially
if compared to the pollution levels tolerated on account of
the presence of foreign tourists. On the other hand a large
number of towns in the South show high percentages of
negative results, a clear sign of a different response to
the problem of pollution on part of local authorities.

From the report of the Ministry of Health it emerges that the factors which determine the unsuitability for bathing of a coastal stretch depend largely on the presence of micro-organisms [6] of faecal origin. (Fig. 4).

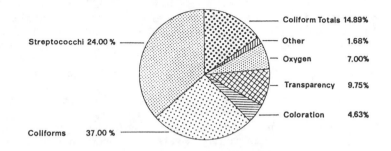

The sector others includes parameters with values below 3%

Fig. 4 -   Sea water at bathing resorts in   1988. Percentage
            indications of pollution using the parameters.
            (Ministry of Health DPR 470/82)

    Such indications underline that pollution is essentially an economic problem and that political powers are not always able to manage it in a suitable way[8] Unauthorised constructions [7], deficiencies in planning inefficiencies in organization - 90% of existing treatment plants are inefficient or non-working (Leone, 1988) - and of personnel [9] easily explain the low quality of the waters in many coastal sectors of the South, where the problem still seems to be irrelevant only because of favourable physical conditions of the sea, which is quite deep and characterised by anti-clockwise currents which push the polluting substances towards the open sea.
    Although they are limited to a few areas, the discharges from the thermo-electric plants can influence changes in the water. The rise in temperature encourages various biological processes with harmful consequences for the ecosystem (Delsoldato, 1987).

Pollution in relation to temporal factors.

    The Italian peninsula has a set of climatic conditions which are determined by its geographical position and its geomorphological particularities.
    Due to these characteristics the pollution of coastal waters shows temporal and positional variations. If we look at the sample data that have been collected, a picture emerges that is strongly influenced by the different

rainfall rate and by the flow rate of the rivers.

While the coastal belt of the Tyrrhenian Sea and that of the Ionian and the middle Adriatic are characterised by a temperate warm climate with a rainfall of 500 - 600mm for year which occurs mostly in winter, the Padana plain and the Alpine belt show the effects of a temperate subcontinental climate with a more consistent rainfall in spring and autumn. It follows that because of the spread of pollution and the washing away effect of rains and also because of the insufficiency of cleaning and emptying operations, the streams carry to the sea large quantities of pollutants during the period of maximum rainfall.

It is worthwhile nevertheless to point out that such occasions end up in a very different reality.

In summer, in the central south of the peninsula the quantity of pollutants is controlled somewhat due to a lack of precipitation and because of the consequent reduced availability of water for domestic and irrigation uses; so that the flow of amounts of pollution towards the sea become considerably slowed down by the low flow rate in the low water courses which are often dried-up. In the centre and above all in the north, even though in the presence of analogous situations concerning precipitation, there are amounts of pollution different in quantity and quality in regard to the greater water availability and to the presence of a large hydrographic network whose flow rate, served by numerous hydroelectric basins, is rather constant. Where as the pollutants of a microbiological origin and of industrial effluents one few, the former because of a widespread sevage treatment plants, the latter because of a reduced working efficiency, rather pronounced are the amounts of agricultural derivation brought about by the intense fertilisation and irrigation carried on in the warmest and most productive period.

Causes, effects and remedies of pollution

From what has been said two general considerations can be made. Firstly the most marked changes come about not when derived from a single source of pollution but rather when added factors (demographic and production increase) and the combining of elements (detergents, effluents, discharges, fertilisers and pesticides) accentuate the size of the phenomenon.

On the other hand, since the environmental deterioration and the problem of waste seem to be almost naturally linked to the economic growth of industrialised countries, in Italy pollution is seen in all its gravity along the coastal belt because of its particular geomorphological conformation. A narrow peninsula in a

north/south direction, it presents a coastal development of
7.052 Kms [10] approximately 50% of which being low and
sandy. If one adds to this that, about 77% of the Italian
mainland can be classified as hilly and mountainous, it is
easily understood how the flat lands (except for the Po
plain) are all located along coasts (Fig.5).

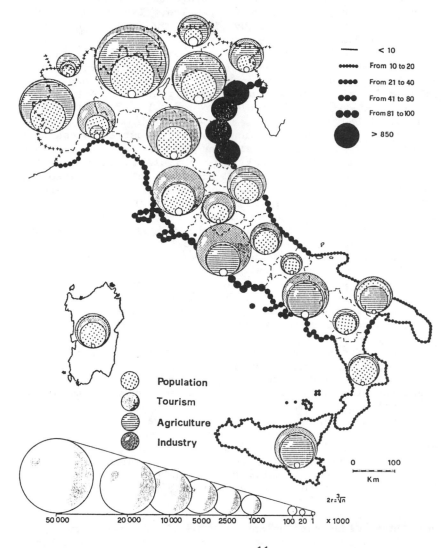

Fig. 5 -   Population Equivalent [11]   per Region and per
            Kilometre of the coast (for agriculture an
            industry based on BOD).

From a situation of low demographic crowding due to morphological features (high coasts) or to the existence of marshlands, and of scattered economic activities organised on poles, in a few decades a completely opposite situation has come about. The economic relations as a result of operations at sea, of the road network and of reclamation of extended marshes have become progressively longitudinal with a pattern centred on nodes (Zunica, 1986), whilst the coast has been affected by increasing demographic and industrial density.

In such a context a process of deterioration accompanied by a rise of pollution was nearly inevitable exactly [12] where diverse economic activities had been allowed, since the effluents, so different in origin and types, had become difficult to control and neutralise. (Zunica, 1988).

Rivers contribute in considerable measure to coastal pollution through mechanical and physico-chemical action. They carry to the sea not[13] only pollutants dispersed in their catchment basin but because of the seasonal variability of their load of water they can generate unbalances in the ecosystems. Because of its different specific weight the water coming from rivers tends to stratify in separate layers. Such a situation, which refors espacially in conditions of calm sea and high temperatures tends now to be a common along low coasts even in relation with the operations that have been set to halt the processes of erosion. The completion of sea works (barriers and defences) tends to retard the wave action and the remixing process, already precarious in a sea like the Mediterranean which takes about eighty years to recycle its waters.

The effects of coastal pollution are getting more and more serious since, with the productive processes and urbanisation bound to create increasing pollution pressures, the autopurification process always becomes more difficult and lengthy.

In this way, phenomena that once were biological and limited in time and space (as the flourishing and increase of algae, gelatine, anoxia) have become more frequent and have originated lots of problems to the marine ecosystem and also to coastal activities, such as those of the tourist industry and fishing for which the sea is their primary resource.

The acknowledged necessity to reduce pollution has not yet found adequate solutions.

The complexity and the diversity of the variables, which contribute to coastal pollution, added to a multiplicity of different organisms with varying biological cycles does not yet allow precise diagnoses and, whith them, accurate remedies.

Because of this the initiatives which can be undertaken to mitigate the phenomena appear to be divided into a series of preventative and recuperative measures.

The preventative action is at the moment the lasiest and the most practicable solution. It should be expressed as a series of prompt measures to reduce at source the pollutant substances deposited directly or indirectly into the sea, by industries (through the recycling of used waters) and by agriculture (through the use of the water cleaned by treatment plants).

More complex solutions with the use of advanced technology and with increasing investment, seem less realistic in the short term.

Operations of salvage and cleansing of waterways and the coastal belt are considered instead in the medium and long term. The priority of these operations is directed without doubt to the rivers [14]. Yet being potential primary sources of pollution for the quantity and quality of drained effluents they only allow preventive action and reclamation in as much as the distribution of urban and industrial discharges is easily identifiable.

The reclamation of the coastal belt turns out to be less easy. The recovery can only be possible when all the operations already put forward have been fulfiled since the reclamation of the marine environment and particularly of the coast can come only from the sea itself and from the autopurification capacity of its own waters.

Conclusions

The sea is a complex ecosystem and the coast, as the interface between land and sea cannot be managed by local administrative operations. The scientific results must be assessed and compared and the actual returns evaluated by means of an overall plan. Regional experts of different ministries of the many Countries which border the Mediterranean sea must find a single policy and a common strategy. To avoid errors and inefficient checks the responsibility for water pollution should be endorsed to a single agency which should be entrusted with the survey of the data and the co-ordination of the operations intended to protect not only the environment but also (and above all) the welfare of mankind.

Yet it is undeniable that such results can be attained only with the support of individuals in as much as they regard the environment and the sea as a resource to be protected and not to be consumed and destroyed. For this reason a change in life-style and in economic and cultural models is indispensable.

Notes

1) Amongst the sources of pollution industry accounts for
29%, agriculture for 22%, population for 43% and nautical
uses for 6%.

2) In the analyses of the conditions of bathing waters,
heavy metals are not considered in connection with a
shortage of proven scientific data about their poisonous
properties. It is nevertheless claimed that, limited
percentages of mercury can provoke inflammation and
blisters on the skin of swimmers; nickel can cause itching,
vascular troubles and in same cases burns, and copper,
lesions of the mucous and conjunctive membranes.

3) The estimates indicate 50 million tons as the quantity
of industrial waste (of which 10% is defined as toxic and
poisonous). This is then added to 16 million tons of solid
urban waste. In fact only 20% of industrial waste is
treated and neutralised.

4) Modern agriculture always needs major quantities of
phosphates and fertilisers. The phosphorus distributed on
the soil of Italy amounts to 400 thousand tons (260 of
chemical fertilisers, the rest of natural origin). Also
considerable is the pollution from zootechnica. In Padana
plain alone breedings of 6 million pigs and of other kinds
of cattle make a pollution load equivalent to a population
of 90 million people. Of this amount two-thirds is used as
fertiliser and the rest is poured directly into rivers.

5) Detergents, have today a very limited role, thanks to
the legal measures which in recent years have compelled
industry to reduce the percentages of powders containing
phosphorus from 8% to 2.5% (from January 1st 1989 to 1%).
If the law has brought about a reduction of phosphorus from
33.2% to 12.7%, it still remains high as a derivative
contribution from metabolic waste at 33.6%, from
agriculture at 29.5%, from zootechnica at 14.1%, from
industry at 7.4% and from uncultivated soils at 2.7%.

6) Amongst the factors which determine the unsuitability of
bathing waters are coliforms occurring at a level of 37%,
total coliforms at 15% streptococchus at 25%. Less relevant
instead are the physical chemical parameters of 9% in the
case of transparency, 7% for oxygen, 5% for colour, and 2%
for the "others".

7) Heavy building is one of the most worrying phenomena
along the coast. Constructions of millions of cubic meters

in size have irremediably changed the landscape and the
environment creating the conditions for microbiological
pollution which consitutes the primary cause of more than
90% of negative evaluations of bathing waters in regions
such as Sicily, Calabria, Basilicata and Campania.

8) The lack of a territorial plan for whole coastal
stretches up to 2kms in depth brings about aberrant
situations. It is sufficient to cite the case of Sardinia
which anticipates the building of second homes with 60
million cubic meters of concrete, the equivalent of a
concrete ring which could rehouse the population of the
whole island but which won't rehouse anyone because they
will all be tourist houses.

9) Sometimes it is about a shortage of personnel but more
often they are negligence, bureaucratica wrangles, long-
established laziness and shortcuts which make the service
inefficient (see for example the result figures per Region
Tab. 1).

10) The length relative to the development of the Italian
coast varies in relation to the exact period when the
survey was carried out (time of artificial replenishing of
land reclamation or of erosion) and also to the various
criteria used (with or without islands) or to the intended
purpose. In this case the reference is to the data given by
the Ministry of Health on the conditions of swimming
waters.

11) The pollutants effects of civil, industrial and
agricultural effluents, mesured in terms of organic
substances (in solution or in suspension) is expressed by
BOD. Through the use of appropriate parameters it is
feasible to correlate population equivalent and the
pollution coming from industrial, agricultural and civil
discharges. It can be defined as a relationship between the
number of inhabitants whose daily domestic refuse uses up a
quantity of oxigen (BOD) and that demand from the
particular effluents in one day. (Southgate, 1948)

12) During the last thirty years the greater economic and
production oportunities of the coastal selvage has brought
an increasing urbanisation: in fact 30% of the population
live in coastal communities, 9 million foreign tourists
take their holidays at the sea in the summer months, 18% of
the national total of industry with around 1.2 million
personnel are concentrated along the coasts. The
significance and consequences of such figures in relation
to the quantity of the pollution put into the sea can be

easily guessed.

13) The pollutant contribution of rivers and streams often caused by urban dumping, as much from the small as the large urban centres of the whole country, are broght down to "collecting" rivers which carry to the sea huge amounts of pollutants. Information relating to such materials carried by the River Po on one summer's day, have been calculated to be 8 quintals of arsenic, 24 of zinc, 20 of chrome, 144 of detergents, 188 of phosphates, 35 of ammonia, 1640 of nitrates, 260 of mineral oils, 40 of lead more than 120 Kgs of pesticides and 172 of mercury.

14) A Committee for the reclamation of the basin of the river Po has been already formed and it as already obteined the first funds by the Italian government.

References

AA.VV.: Atti 33° Congresso Nazionale della S.I.I.M.P.S.P., C.I.C Edizioni Int., Milano, (1988).

Berbenni, P. - Galassi, G.: Chimica ed ecologia delle acque, Etas Libri, Milano, pp. 9, 40,194, (1978).

Greco, N.: Gestione e tutela delle coste e delle acque costiere in Italia, "Ambiente risorse salute", 34, III, vol. XI, pp. 4-6 (1984).

Lega Ambiente: Operazione Goletta Verde 87, Coop. Ecologia, Roma (1988).

Leone, U.: Geografia per l'ambiente, N.I.S, Roma, p. 79, (1987).

Martinis, B.: Geologia ambientale, UTET, Torino, p. 109, (1988).

Ministero della Sanità: Rapporto sulla qualità delle acque di balneazione - anni 1987-1986-1985-1984, Centro Stampa Serv. Centr. Programm. Sanitaria, Roma, (1988).

Southgate, B.A.: Treatment and disposal of industrial Water Wastes His Majesty's Stationary Office, London, (1948).

Zunica, M.: Lo spazio costiero italiano, V. Levi Ed., Roma, pp. 136-142, (1987).

Zunica, M.: Per un approccio con l'interfaccia terra-mare, "Quad. Dip. Geogr. Univ. Padova", 5, pp. 10-11, (1987).

Degradation of Coastal Dune Systems Through Anthropogenic Action

Carlo Cencini* and Luigi Varani*

Abstract

The paper describes the impact of human activities on the extensive system of dunal ridges which, up to last century, fringed entirely the sandy beaches of Italy.

The reasons for man-induced modifications were numerous: construction of railways, land reclamations, pine-woods planting, tourist development and pressure of recreational activities. These combined factors have converged toward a rapid deterioration of the coastal environment. Dunes have been flattened or erased to provide sand for concrete, to build hotels and condominiums, to make way for recreational practices or easier access to the beach and so on.

In order to give an overview of these changes, the discussion is focused on seven selected coastal sectors.

An historical overview

The outline of Italian coasts (main islands included) has been defining during the last six millennia, when the stabilization of sea level after Holocene transgression favoured alluvial deposition along shore.

During historical times siltation processes were particularly evident expecially along low sandy beaches and in connection with deltaic formations and were conditioned, without any doubt, by human activities in the hinterland (Delano Smith, 1979).

Sedimentological as well as archaeological and historical evidences corroborate this hypothesis. Remains of settlements and harbours of Roman and Greek age document the progradation of many coasts. Examples are numerous and include Pisa, Ravenna, Ostia, Luni, Cuma, Sibari, Metaponto, and so on: all of these had been originally important ports sited along the sea-front or in the vicinity of river outlets, whereas they presently lie at some distance landwards from the shore.

During recent centuries and particularly since the 1700s, flooding processes have been particularly intense as a result of an unprecedented increase in population and consequent deforestation and tillage in mountain areas, especially in the Apennines.

_____

*Associated Professors, Department of Geography, University of Bologna, Bologna (Italy)

Evidences can be deduced from topographic maps of 18th and 19th centuries which show an accelerating growth of deltaic cusps and adjacent beaches.

The retrait of the sea left space to the development of extensive dune systems and sand ridges, whose disposition shows the sequence of the evolutionary trend. At the same time, the depressions between the bars and the alluvial plains, were occupied in many cases by inland lakes, salt-lagoon systems or marshlands.

Still at the half of last century, almost the entire length of sandy beaches of Italy was bordered by a strip of dunes, which endowed the landscape with characteristic features. Dune ridges - favoured by low gradients of the sea floor and a very limited influence of tidal currents - were particularly numerous in the vicinities of major river outlets or anywhere drift supplied enough nourishment of sediment to the beaches.

The form and the dimension of coastal dunes were considerably varied, as determined by interaction between natural processes and sand source. Usually they reached 5-10 m in height (but in some stretches 20-30 m was also common), formed long bars parallel to the shoreline and occupied an area of width ranging between some hundred metres to a few kilometers.

Foredunes were live and colonized by a typical succession of psammophyle vegetation (Corbetta et al., 1984), which afforded an efficient obstacle to sand trasportation and played an important role in dune building. Inland ridges were consolidated by Mediterranean scrub (macchia) or by native woods.

Evidence for the presence of man was scarce and natural processes were still prevailing in the modelling of the shore. Up to the last century, little or no interest was taken in the coastal strip, too often marshy, malarious and unfavourable for settlement. Along shore, economic activities were limited to hunting, fishing and some marginal form of grazing, as transhumance.

But dunes are fragile landforms that could be easily degraded by human activities or displaced by natural processes. In fact, the human impact on Italian coastlands over the last century has quickly destroyed these ecosystems, whose formation man itself had indireclty contributed in previous times.

Recent transformations

One of the first impacts of man on the dune systems took place in the second half of last century with the developing of railways which, in a mountainous country like Italy, were established mostly along coast. The first Adriatic railroad was constructed in the 1860's directly over the low dune ridges which backed the coastline of Marche and Abruzzi. In the same way, further railways were established over the dunes of the Gulf of Taranto or along the Tyrrhenian coast of Tuscany and Latium.

Nevertheless these transformations were not the main agents in terms of destruction: coastlands were still uncoltivated and pratically deserted.

Another push toward the alteration of dune systems was brought about by very extensive operations of reclamation, which started around the turn of this century with the aim of eradicating the endemy of malaria and also of gaining new farming land.

Along with reclamation, pine-woods began to be planted over dunar ridges which edged the coastal plains, with the aim of protecting inland crops from sea-winds. This technique, common in many Italian coastlands, was encouraged through legislative measures, which led to the purchase on part of the government of vast areas for reforestation.

In this way many stretches of Italian coastline (like along the coasts of Tuscany, Latium, Campania, Emilia-Romagna, Friuli, etc) were fringed by artificial woods, mostly stone- and cluster-pines (*Pinus pinea, P. pinaster, P. halepensis*) which undoubtedly played a useful role also in terms of dune consolidation and shore protection.

However these species of pines are not native ones and their artificial woods are unstable and fragile communities, which frequently suffered heavy damages from sandy, salty and recently also polluted sea-winds.

The main factor of degradation or destruction of dunes was undoubtedly the development of recreational uses along the sea-side. Facilities for recreation started to appear along some Italian coasts since the turn of the century, but only after World War II the spread of mass-tourism involved the major part of coastal areas and stimulated a very heavy demand for waterfront.

Favoured by lack of regulations and protection, roads, hotels, condominiums and other large buildings were located directly over back-dunes, which were almost totally destroyed. Front dunes, which normally lie between the beach and the buildings were also flattened to make way for the *bagni* (bath-houses) and easier access to the beaches, notwithstanding the fact that in Italy to these areas are governmental properties.

Also dunes not directly involved with housing were often impacted heavily: they were mined to provide cheap sand for concrete; scarred by uncontrolled camping and parking or devegetated by footpaths and vehicular traffic.

These activities often lead to further dune destruction by increasing the amount of wind erosion, so at present relic foredunes are lowered and affected by numerous breaches and rarely provide a good protection for the shore. The damage of dune formations was often accompanied by the alteration of dunar vegetation or the disappearance of coastal pine-forests.

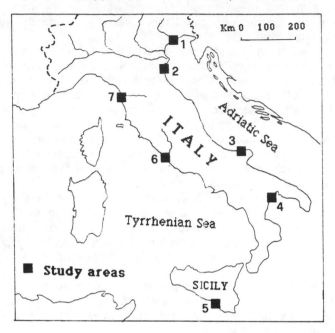

Fig.1. Location of study areas.

Some case studies
The total length of the non-cliffy coastline of Italy is about 3500 km, so the discussion will focus on seven different coastal sectors selected among the most significant ones (Fig.1).

Evidence for the transformations which have occurred in these areas comes by comparing different editions of topographic maps as well as aerial photographs. From these sources, we have drawn simplified maps underlining the most significat evolutionary trends.

1. The Tagliamento Delta - The Tagliamento River, which flows to the northern shores of the Adriatic Sea, has produced a typical symmetrical two-winged delta, elongated for about 15 km and enlarged up to 4 km in its apex.

This is a good example of a complex system of dunes which clearly evidence the continuity of the delta formation. Old maps reveal the extent and the importance of the sand ridges: the dunes were 8-10 m high and extended on both side of the river mouth, ranging 8 to 15 arch-shaped ridges.

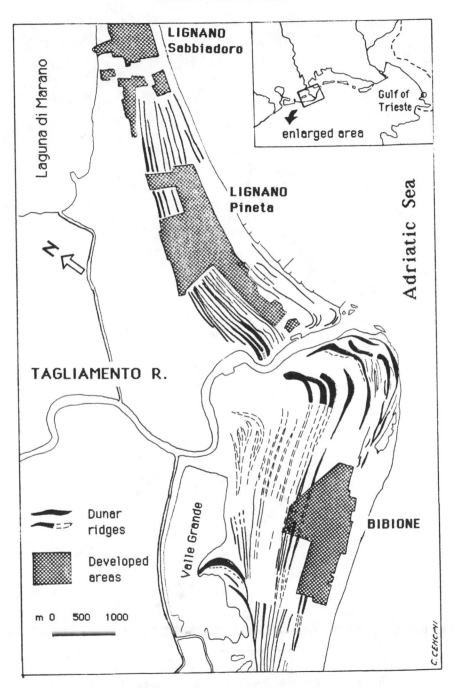

Fig. 2. Relic dunar ridges in the Tagliamento river delta

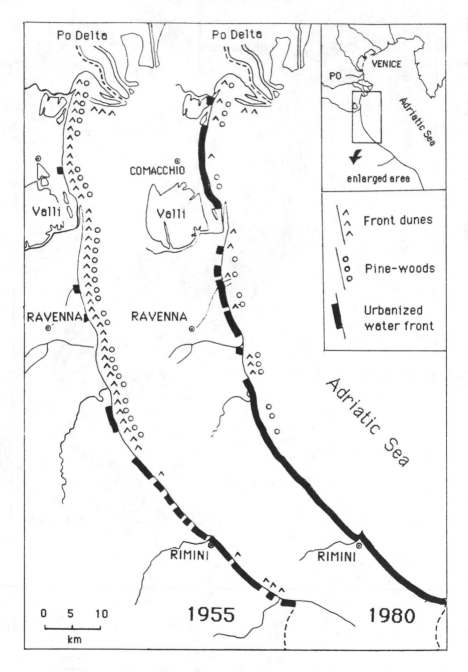

Fig. 3. The coast of Emilia-Romagna. Impact of urbanization on pine-woods and front dunes: 1955 and 1980.

Up to World War II the development of tourism in this site was delayed in relation to difficult access over the extensive marshes north of the delta. However once tourism entered the scene, several sea-side resorts were developed during the last decades: Lignano Sabbiadoro and Lignano Pineta to the left of the river outlet, Bibione and Bibione Pineda to the right.

Built-up areas, extending for about 700 hectares, support a tourist attendance (in terms of number of visitors multiplied by days of stay) of about 5 millions per year on each side of the delta.

Inevitably the tourist pressure has resulted in a drastic change in existing ecosystems; in particular in the dune area, which has decreased by more than half over the last 25 years (Fig. 2).

2. The flat coast south of the Po Delta - The flat coast of Emilia-Romagna has been associated with the development of river outlets which had been prograding through the marshes and the lagoons fringing the coast. At the end of the nineteenth-century this coastal stretch was mostly repulsive for settlement, but, in less than a century, man has gained firm possession of this land almost to the point of erasing its natural features.

In the 1950's, two thirds of the coast of Emilia-Romagna was already developed and transformed into the most extensive coastal conurbation of the country. By the 1960's the urban growth involved the remaining coast leading to almost complete deterioration of the natural landscape, as dune areas and woodlands.

Over the last 25 years the dune-occupied surface (including back-dunes consolidated by pine-woods) has decreased by more than a half. However, the most serious damages was suffered by foredunes, whose area has been reduced to less than a quarter.

More data give a clearer picture of the transformation: in 1955, 60 km of the regional coastline were bordered by dunes, against the 20 of 1980 (Cencini 1980) (Fig. 3). However even figures do not give a complete picture if we consider that dunar barrier, even where it still exists, is rarely a good defence against winds, erosion or sea floading related with high tides (*acqua alta*).

3. The dunes of Lesina (Gargano) - In the northern coast of the Gargano (Southern Adriatic), the sediments of the Fortore river have nourished two long littoral spits which enclose the coastal lakes of Lesina and Varano. The sand bar enclosing the Lesina lake is occupied by a well developed system of dunes, extended from Punta Pietre Nere to Torre Milelu, for a length of more than 20 km, with a width decreasing from W to E and a total surface of about 1400 hectares.

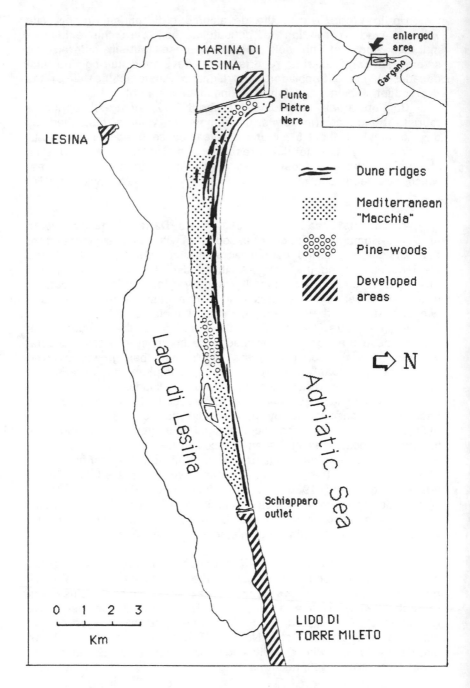

Fig. 4. Lake of Lesina: significant land uses

This stretch is a good example showing the sharp contrast between a sector still in good environmental conditions (the western one from Punta Pietre Nere to the Schiapparo outlet) and a contiguous one heavily degraded (from Schiapparo to Torre Mileto) (Fig. 4).

The heavy deterioration of the natural ecosystem in the eastern sector is the result of a chaotic spread of touristic urbanization along a waterfront of 5 km in length, close to Torre Mileto. Here housing took place without any control nor compliance to regulations, directly over dune ridges, which were totally flattened. The new settlements, in spite of lack of any infrastructural works (like roads, aqueducts, drains, electricity) host in the summer over 30000 people.

Instead, the western sector is a relative natural landscape and it is protected by a natural preserve. However the first signs of land movement operations (beach accesses, spaces for camping) imply further urban growth of Marina di Lesina eastward on the foredunes which are moreover damaged by erosion.

4. The Gulf of Taranto - The coastline of the Gulf of Taranto extends in a gentle arc some 60 km along the Jonian Sea. Archaeological sites testify heavy sedimentation and rapid progradation along beaches during historical times. The rich sediment load carried by several torrents (such as Lato, Bradano, Basento, Cavone, Agri, Sinni) favoured the growth of a vast and huge system of dunes. Early maps clearly show the extent and importance of such formations: 10 to 20 m in height, shaped in long bars parallel to the coastline, the dunes fringed a long and narrow alluvial plane once marshy and recently reclamed.

At present these areas are generally well preserved, but signs of anthropogenic degradation are present. Some of these are shown in Fig. 5 which illustrates the coastal stretch between Lato and Basento outlets. Here three different kinds of man-induced modifications of the coastal environment can be identified.

The first massive impact was due to the construction of the railway close to the coast in the second half of last century.

A second stage of alteration involves the extensive reclamation projects carried on during the 1950-60's, which not only increased the land available to agriculture but also reduced the area occupied by back-dunes.

Finally the recreational pressure during the last few decades favoured the development of new sea-side resorts in the area Thus about 500 hectares of dunes were flattened to provide space for the new built-up areas of Castellaneta Marina, Riva dei Téssali, Marina di Ginosa and Metaponto Lido.

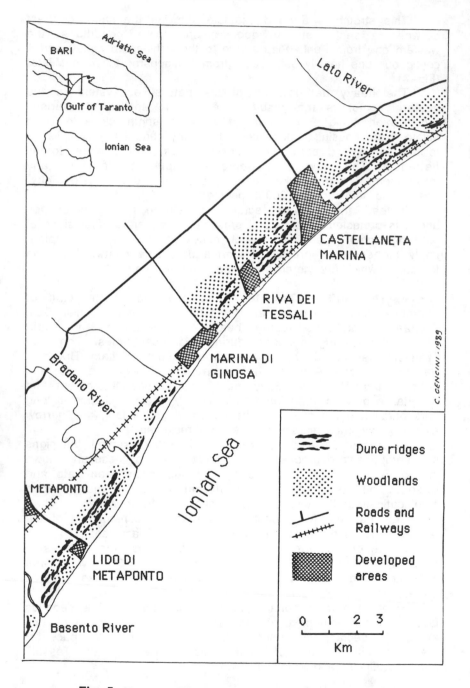

Fig. 5 New sea-side resorts along the Gulf of Taranto

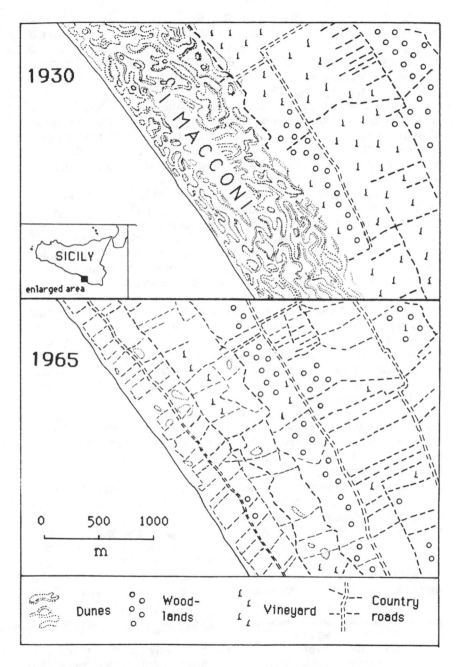

1930

SICILY

enlarged area

I MACCONI

1965

0 500 1000

m

Dunes

Wood-
lands

Vineyard

Country
roads

Fig. 6 "I Macconi" (Sicily). Recent agricultural uses of dunes

5. "I Macconi" (Southern Sicily) - *I Macconi* is the local name of a coastal stretch of Southern Sicily, which extends along a front of about 11 km in length and an average width of about 900 m, between the Acate outlet and Punta Zaffaglione. This is a good example of destruction of a whole dune system to provide space for specialized farming (Fig. 6).

In the area, up to the 1930's, dunes where still a basic feature of the landscape; there were shaped in relatively isolated masses of huge dimension (20-30 m in height usually) and running roughly parallel to the coast, but sometime rather obliquely to it. There was a sharp contrast between this area and the district behind the dunes, already cultivated and settled.

On this area by the 1960's the new agricultural assett has deeply changed the coastal landscape: recently gained lands display a regular grid pattern created by the construction of a country road crossed by a thick net-work of rural tracks. Morphologic modifications were dramatic: the dunar system had almost totally levelled or reduced in height and the few surviving dunes are now interspersed by agricultural practices and greenhouses.

6-7. The Tiber and the Arno Deltas - The two major rivers which drain the Apennine - the Tiber and Arno - flow into the Tyrrhenian sea. As a result of the high erodibility of their basins and of extensive deforestation carried out in the uplands, these deltas have undergone a rapid progradation during historical times, resulting in the formation of relatively wide coastal planes.

Early maps show that in the past deltaic forelands - uncoltivated, swampy, and partly covered by native scrub - were bordered on the waterfront by several dunar ridges extended over an area sometimes ranging 5 km in width. The dunes were locally called *tumuleti* along the coast of Latium (Tiber delta) and *tomboli* along the Tuscan one (Arno outlet).

These once deserted areas early developed into spaces functional to recreational or residential purposes. In the 1920's Lido di Ostia was already well attended as a sea-side resort for the middle class of Rome. After World War II, the whole coastal area in front of Rome was faced with heavy urbanization, in connection with the vicinity of the city. Thus on both sides of the Tiber outlet, for approximately 25 km, dunes were totally flattened to make space for buildings, condominiums and recreational activities. They still persist only along some stretches facing the residual pine-woods of Castel Fusano and Castel Porziano, while elsewere they appear heavily damaged (Fig. 7).

Quite similar were the processes involving the numerous *tomboli* located to the south of the Arno outlet, where since the turn of the century Marina di Pisa was established , one of the

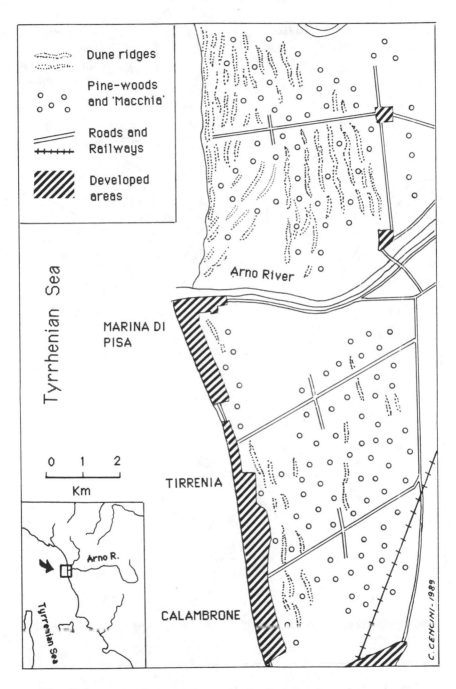

Fig. 7. Dunar system and touristic development in the Arno delta.

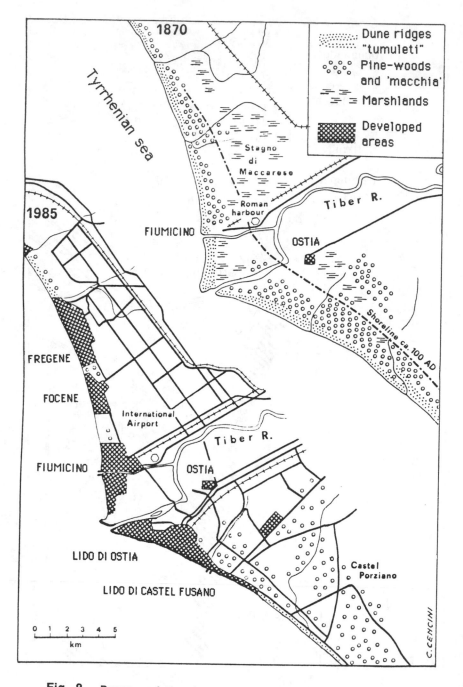

Fig. 8. Dunar evolution in the Tiber Delta during last century

earliest coastal settlement for recreational purposes in the country. Later the progressing urbanization of the southern waterfront (with the establishment of the new resorts of Tirrenia and Calambrone) caused the disappearance of foredunes for about 10 km.

The northern sector of the delta, on the contrary, has little human disturbance: the presence of a national natural preserve helps to maintain morphologic and vegetational features. The only damages to the dune system are due to beach erosion which, during the last few decades, has been extremely heavy (Fig. 8).

References

Caputo, C.; D'Alessandro, L.; La Monica, G.B.; Landini, B.; Lupia Palmieri, E.; Pugliese, F.: Erosion problems on the coast of Lazio (Italy). In Bird, E.C.F.; Fabbri, P. (eds), Coastal problems in the Mediterranean Sea, pp. 59-68. CCE-IGU, Bologna, 1983.

Cencini, C.: L'evoluzione delle dune del litorale romagnolo nell'ultimo secolo. CCIAA, Forlì 1980.

Corbetta, F.; Puppi, G.; Speranza, M.; Zanotti, A.L.: Vegetational Outlines of North Adriatic Coast. Acta Bot. Croat. 43, 191-206 (1984)

Delano Smith, C.: Western Mediterranean Europe. A historical geography of Italy, Spain and Southern France since the Neolithic. Academic Press, Londra,1979.

Gandolfi, G.; Mordenti, A.; Paganelli, L.: Spiagge attuali e cordoni di dune nell'area del delta del Tagliamento e di Valle Vecchia. Miner. Petrogr. Acta 22, 95-110 (1978)

Landini, P.; Leone, V.: Ipotesi di un parco naturale nella duna di Lesina: un approccio interdisciplinare. Mem. Soc. Geogr. Ital.,33, 483-501 (1984)

Marinas and Minor Harbors in the Northern Adriatic

Giuseppe Rizzo *

Abstract

Recreational boating has been a significant factor in the expansion of tourism in the Northern Adriatic coast in the 1970s and particularly in more recent years. This paper focuses on three different kinds of harbors, according to physical features (lagoon, river and coastline), analysed into their water surface area, moorings available, facilities and services. Pleasure craft users are studied in the light of their distance from marinas, interactions with seaside resorts and their leisure habits. By the analysis one may rely on gravitative models for smaller harbors whereas this does not seem to be the case for larger ones.

Introduction

    Pleasure boating, limited and elitist up to the end of the 1960s, experienced in the following decade a considerable boom in Italy which, notwithstanding certain fluctuations, has lasted up to the present. This was the result of an increase in leisure time caused by social evolution, the levelling of standard of living, the widespread increase of income, the perception of yachting as a less exclusive pastime and the appearance on the market of boats more accessible to the general public and which can be easily towed. All these factors explain the evolution of this particular type of tourism and justify the prediction that its diffusion will continue(1). This is also being stimulated by psychological factors such as the acquisition of a higher social status, the need for adventure, contact with nature and the quest for emotional experiences and sensations outside the routine of everyday life.
    Boating for leisure has thus reached a large diffusion - it is estimated that the number of boats in Italy amounted to approximately 675.000 in 1986 (Ucina-Consornautica,1987) - and although it was to be considered in the tourism supply as the whole, it has now obtained its own particular status(2). In addition to small-time boating, made possible by vessels little enough to be moved

* Associate Professor of Economic Geography, Institute of Geography, University of Verona, via dell'Artigliere 19, 37129 Verona, Italy.

on a car trailer (an activity almost exclusively limited to
coastal day trips) there are also larger vessels with
cabins and certain comforts, which require a certain degree
of seamanship and hence imply an industrial production
(Bonora, 1984). The latter rather than the former calls for
forms of tourism different from traditional ones, based on
land accommodation. By contrast, the points of reference on
land, needed by boaters, cannot be anything other than
harbors and its facilities. For small-time boating
(applicable to crafts under 7 meters - 80% of Italian
boats), which tends to occupy mooring spaces in clusters
rather than at single points, very simple structures are
sufficient and these may be in close integration with the
beach. However for various reasons they are often moored on
the waterfront like larger boats(3).

Despite significant differences in nature, needs,
utilization, compatibility with other activities and types
of users both small-time and large-time boating are
important because they exert a great influence on the
development of the coastland (Rizzo, 1986).

Both have indeed contributed to greater diversification
in tourist activities, introducing new attractions and
sometimes even determining the construction of new
residential areas, in some cases closed off from the
surroundings (Valussi, 1986).

To understand the pattern of territorial structuring
related to yachting it is necessary to survey not only the
urban and environmental consequences and the problems of
accessibility, but also the patterns of fluctuation, the
places of origin and the multiplier effect on the local
economy, to mention only a few of the most important
aspects. These are the aims of this research, carried out
along the Northern Adriatic coastline between the outlets
of the Po River and the Italo-Yugoslav border which are
under the administration of the Veneto and Friuli-Venezia
Giulia Regions.

The Environment

For leisure boating, as for any other form of tourism,
geographical conditions play a fundamental role in making a
place attractive and in determining the location of its
facilities. Natural features are of primary importance
when, as is the case of yachting tourism, they not only
help to create a pleasant environment but also determine
whether or not tourists can enjoy the activities they have
sought. A brief outline (Brambati,1987 and 1988; Zunica
1971 and 1985) of the physical features of the Northern
Adriatic coast seems therefore appropriate (fig.1)

The coastline in the Veneto region is curved, its
concavity facing WNW-ESE. It extends for 145 Kilometers
from the outlet of Po di Goro to the Tagliamento river and
is made up of gently sloping sandy beaches of various
width. At one time the coast was bordered by dunes and pine
woods, but these have been significantly reduced by human
intervention. The coastline is often interrupted by inlets,
marshes, fishing waters in the Po delta and outlets of
waterways and of lagoons which blur the distinction between

sea and land. Even further inland, sea and land are
interconnected: besides   the Po delta we can find the
lagoons of Venice and of Caorle and the delta of
Tagliamento.

The gentle slope of the beaches continues into the sea
(the bathymetry usually only reads -5 meters at a distance
of 1,000 or more meters from the shoreline) where a large
number of sand bars are to be found.

The   Friuli-Venezia   Giulia   coastline,   about   81
kilometres in length, is less developed and can be divided
into two sections, from the Tagliamento outlet to the
Timavo and from there to the national border.

The first is a fine sinuous sandy coastline with gentle
slopes which are facing hidden barriers more or less out at
sea, behind which the lagoons of Grado and Marano extend:
conditions very similar to those of the beaches in Veneto.
The second section is made up of a rather high cliff in its
first part, then it becomes smoother scattered with
alluvial plains. This part anticipates the characteristics
of the Istrian and Dalmatian coastlands of Yugoslavia,
which are rugged and fringed by festoons of islands.

Fair weather conditions for sailing usually prevail
during the summer months. Wind speeds vary at different
points along the coast although, along the whole stretch,
offshore and sea breezes play a more significant part.
Underwater currents vary according to the features of the
coastline but their speed, except for areas overlooking
river or lagoon outlets, is not particularly notable. Even
the tides do not usually range over 0.2 meters; only in
extremes do they approach 1 meter.

It is necessary to stress, however, the notable
presence of pennants, jetties, dams and reefs which provide
protection, at least in part, against erosion. The area is
intensely populated and this has been encouraged by the
advent of mass tourism. For the most part, these are
foreign tourists and the points of highest concentration
are the beaches.

To the attractions offered by these places to beach
tourists and small-time boaters we must add the presence of
Venice, Trieste and many other minor coastal and inner
towns.

Harbor Structures

The littoral can be divided on the basis of its
geographical character into the following five sections:

- Veneto Region

a) from the outlet of Po di Goro mouth to the outlet of
   Brenta river - number 1 to 6 in fig.1 and table 3;
b) the Lagoon of Venice - number 7 to 28;
c) from Porto di Lido to the outlet of Tagliamento
   river - number 29 to 39;

- Friuli - Venezia Giulia Region

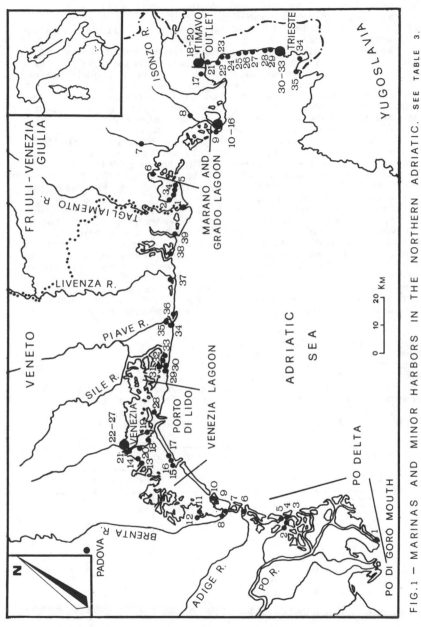

FIG. 1 — MARINAS AND MINOR HARBORS IN THE NORTHERN ADRIATIC. SEE TABLE 3.

d) the Lagoon of Grado and Marano and the littoral up to
the Timavo river - number 1 to 20;
e) from the outlet of Timavo up to the Italo-Yugoslav
border - number 21 to 35;
    Because of the physiographical features of this coast
the location of the structures is possible only at the
outlets of waterways or on the shore of the lagoons which
are navigable along their major channels. The presence of
underwater barriers makes it difficult in rough sea
conditions, especially for larger vessel, to go out to sea
or come back to port even through the waterways.
    We have classified twenty-four structures as being
situated at the mouths of waterways or canals; thirty-five
in lagoon or similar areas and fifteen are directly on the
coast. The location of structures in three particular kinds
of sites implies different opportunities and difficulties
such as safety, accessibility, distance to the sea and
availability of space(4).
    The large number of harbors results in an average
distance between them of 6-7 kms if we consider only those
located on the waterfront or in its immediate vicinity. For
reasons already mentioned, smaller harbors are usually
clustered together.In any case the distance is short and
allows even for smaller boats to make crossings along
routes that are partly in open sea and partly in waterways.
There is, in fact, a series of canals connecting rivers to
lagoons, which allows for navigation along the back part of
the shore from the mouth of the Po di Goro up to the lagoon
of Grado.
    The structures surveyed present marked differences not
only because of their location but also for the number of
moorings, the surface of water basin, the ratio between
this and the whole area of the harbor, the standard of
facilities offered and the type of management(5).
    As far as dimension is concerned the marinas of Veneto
are on average smaller than those in the other Region.

Table 1. Marinas by water surface and Region

Surface of water	N. Marinas	
(m²)	Veneto	Friuli-Venezia G.
0 - 1,000	3	3
1,001 - 5,000	19	9
5,001 - 10,000	5	5
10,001 - 30,000	8	5
30,001 - 60,000	2	6
60,000 - 100,000	1	4
> 100,000	1	3

Indeed not only do 60% of the Veneto marinas occupy an area of less than 5,000 m² (and 73% less than 3,000 m²) but they hardly ever measure more than 30,000 m² unlike two-thirds of the harbor structures to be found in Friuli-Venezia Giulia. However, this has to be seen in the context of other factors. In the latter region the greater availability of land, once unused because of marshes and poor accessibility, has led to the coupling of harbors with residential quarters which, on account of the huge amount of capital required, could only be of considerable size. This was also influenced by the fact that they were situated near the more attractive Yugoslavian coastline, which requires boats of larger dimension, built for longer cruising and by the continued presence of foreigners particularly Germans, amongst the more wealthy users.

The increase in tourism - with a strong foreign element(6) - on the beaches in the two regions and the diversification of the same has resulted in a strong incentive for a creation of marinas.

If we limit the analysis to the more efficient marinas recently constructed by private investors it is necessary to point out that compared to the building of only thirteen harbors before 1970 no fewer than twenty were built after that date: seven out of ten of these can be considered real and proper nautical centers on account of their structures, size of facilities and the fact that they are closely linked with residential areas. The best ones are located on the coast between the Porto di Lido and Grado where beach tourism is better organized and has been established longer(7) (Gomiscech, 1987).

Plate 1 - Marinas and minor harbors on the Sile outlet (Veneto) (see Table 3 - Numbers 29; 30; 31; 32)

If we consider the ratio between the area of water
basin and the total area we can see in Veneto for more than
half of the harbors (i. e. 20) that it ranges from 1 to 2,
for 10 of them between 2 and 4 and the rest can be
classified at successive intervals up to the value of 9.

Even though 12 of the 20 show a ratio of less than 2
and have a surface basin of not less than 5,000 m², these
values do not strictly correlate with the dimensions of the
harbor; higher ratios are actually found in smaller
harbors.

This can be explained by the fact that major
structures, used by more demanding customers and larger
vessels, are forced to widen their areas as much as
possible; this does not happen as much with smaller units
in which harbor services are regarded as complementary to
other activities such as the servicing and sale of boats.

A comparable situation is to be found up to the Timavo
outlet.

Another significant element is the number of mooring
places available. This depends significantly on how the
harbor is structured, number of landing stages, space to
manoeuver, types and numbers of access routes and above all
the size of the most dominant boats.

Marinas which have less then 150 mooring places amount
to 70% in the coast of Veneto and just 40% in Friuli-
Venezia Giulia (table 2).

Less than 150 moorings and 10,000 m² of water surface
seems to detect less equipped harbors in comparison with
the best ones(8).

Table 2. Marinas by moorings and Region

N. Moorings	N. Marinas	
	Veneto	Friuli-Venezia G.
0 - 50	9	8
51 - 150	18	7
151 - 350	9	12
351 - 600	3	4
> 600	--	4

Shortage of space and a lack of facilities can be
noticed in 12 harbors of Veneto and in 21 of Friuli-Venezia
Giulia. This is, in some degree, due to the fact that we
can find here most of the public marinas and smaller
harbors in which moorings are licensed directly to users by
public boards.

The remaining harbors are managed under government
licence by private enterprise (individuals or groups) and
are therefore sensitive to customer's needs.

T A B L E 3 - LIST OF MARINAS AND MINOR HARBORS

Veneto Region	Surface of water m² (1)	Moorings (2)	1 / 2	Location
Po di Goro mouth - Brenta outlet				
1 -Porto Barricata	4,000	150	27	R
2 -Marina Nuova di Porto Levante	2,500	150	17	R
3 -Approdo Porto Levante	1,040	45	23	R
4 -Darsena Porto Levante	5,700	130	44	R
5 -Albarella	90,760	500	182	L
6 -Porto Fossone	1,500	60	25	R
Lagoon of Venice				
7 -Brenta Service Boat*	3,000	85	35	R
8 -Marina di Brondolo*	4,280	118	36	R
9 -Darsena Montecarlo	1,050	37	28	L
10-Darsena Mosella	2,000	140	14	L
11-Romea Boat Service	2,000	100	20	R
12-Marina di Valli	14,000	320	44	R
13-Darsena Fusina	14,750	160	92	L
14-Nautica Gazzetta	220	20	11	R
15-VenMar	5,160	60	86	L
16-Serenissima	3,000	45	67	L
17-Marina degli Alberoni	1,500	40	38	L
18-Compagnia della Vela	4,000	65	62	L
19-Diporto Velico	20,000	200	100	L
20-Tronchetto	1,500	90	17	L
21-Dalla Pietà Nautica Venezia	3,800	75	51	L
22-Darsena Milan	-	100	-	L
23-Amadi	500	50	10	L
24-Venier	1,500	50	30	L
25-Scafo Club	3,000	40	75	L
26-Darsena D.E.C.	10,000	120	83	L
27-Marina di Campalto	21,000	200	105	L
28-Marina di Lio Grando	9,345	190	49	L
Porto di Lido - Tagliamento outlet				
29-Darsena Faro di Jesolo	4,500	140	32	R
30-Marina del Faro	3,500	100	35	R
31-Marina del Cavallino	25,000	300	83	R
32-Marina di Jesolo	14,000	220	63	R
33-Porto Turistico di Jesolo	40,000	500	80	R
34-Nautica Boat Service	2,500	88	28	R
35-Marina di Cortellazzo	6,000	140	43	R
36-Mariclea Club	11,000	200	55	L
37-Marina "4"	39,000	400 250**	98	R
38-Porto Falconara	600	30	20	L
39-Porto Baseleghe	140,000	300	47	L

Friuli-Venezia Giulia Region

Lagoon of Marano and Grado and Littoral up to Timavo outlet

```
1 -Marina Uno                            33,000     435      76     R
2 -Aprilia Marittima                    130,000    1000     130     L
                                                    240**
3 -Porto dei Residenti                   10,000     166      60     L
4 -Darsena Demaniale                     40,000     320     125     L
5 -Marina di Punta Faro                 150,000     630     238     L
6 -Marano Lagunare                       62,000      50***          L
7 -Cantieri Marina di S.Giorgio          40,000     270     148     R
8 -Marina Di Aquileia                    40,000     290     134     R
9 -Marina S.Vito                         21,000     160     131     S
10-Porto Canale                               -     520       -     L
11-Scuola Vela Austriaca Klinzer          5,000      40     125     L
12-Canottieri Ausonia                     5,000      40     125     L
13-Cantiere Dal Tin                         600      10      60     L
14-Circolo Nautico S.Marco               20,000      65     308     L
15-Ditta Raugna                           1,000      20      50     L
16-S.T.A. Le Cove        .               10,000     100     100     L
17-Marina Hannibal                       40,000     400     100     L
18-Penisola della vela                   15,000     400      38     L
19-Canale Valentinis  .                  27,000     250     108     R
20-Lisert                                 5,000     120      42     R
```

Timavo outlet - The Italo-Jugoslav border

```
21-Villaggio del Pescatore               80,000    1100      73     R
22-Duino                                  2,000      43      47     S
23-Sistiana                              98,000     256     382     S
24-Filtri di Aurisina                     1,800      30      60     S
25-Cannovello de' Zoppoli                   500      14      38     S
26-S.Croce di Trieste                     4,000     100      40     S
27-Grignano                               2,000     310      65     S
28-Cedas                                  2,700      71      38     S
29-Barcola                               10,000     249      40     S
30-Trieste-Canal Grande                   5,600     300      19     S
31-    "      -Sacchetta                 100,000     800     125     S
32-    "      -Porto Lido-Molo F.B.       34,000      90     378     S
33-    "      -S.Sabba                     4,000      70      57     S
34-Muggia                                18,000     270      67     S
35-S.Bartolomeo-Lazzaretto                5,700     154      37     S
```

* Situated on Brenta river gravitating to a lagoon
** Excluding moorings connected to residences
*** Of the 300 moorings only 50 are available for nautical
tourism
R = River or Canal   L = Lagoon   S = Sea

Boat Users

Careful consideration has to be given to the clientele,
their number, the place of origin, how often they use
boats, and related characteristics.
The term "inadequate" when it refers to certain harbors
may lose its negative meaning when structures and
facilities are related to their customers. Users of sailing
boats or small crafts capable of being towed by cars do not

need the some types of equipment and facilities necessary to customers with more demanding boats.

As far as the request for mooring berths is concerned, it has to be pointed out that the demand almost always exceeds the supply. This explains the existence of unlicensed structures, especially in the area between Grado and the Timavo, in the Lagoon of Venice and in the Po delta.

Repeated surveys bring into evidence that the more local the customers are the smaller the harbors; in this case portable boats in particular are the greatest number (9).

The national and regional clientele increases along with the dimension and level of services, since they often have larger vessels and are more likely to be found the more we move Eastward. Likewise foreign boat users increase and make up between 50-60% in the most developed sectors. This is related to accessibility, which is with no doubt better for the sections between Porto di Lido and the outlet of the Timavo. Here main roads can be used as well as motorways and railroads, which run parallel and close to the coast. By contrast, connections to the Po delta can only be made through minor roads. Little harbors, in the inner margins of the lagoons, are difficult to reach from the open sea.

Other interesting aspects are the presence of boats in the harbor and the period of their use. What is clear from interviewing is that the majority (about 55%) use their boats only in summer whereas 30% use them throughout the whole year. Among the latter group there is a prevalence of larger boats like cabin cruisers whereas the towable and open boats are used more in the summer. As far as permanence in the harbor is concerned, about half of the boats remain in the same harbor in the winter: a percentage that increases if we add dry-docked boats. Among these we find nearly all the larger cabin crafts, sailing boats as well as motor cruisers. The percentage drops to about a third for those that are used only in the summer. Of these a net percentage of 30% of portable boats are maintained at the owners' residences.

Minor harbors used by smaller boats reduce their activity considerably during the less favorable months, whereas it only declines slightly in the bigger structures. Because of the type of users and the periods of use, the former are not motivated to take up services which are superfluous and incapable of attracting wealthy clients because of poor accessibility or an environment which is not particularly stimulating from a naturalistic point of view or on the basis of tourist organization as a whole.

Marinas which are better positioned (among them all major ones and those which are better equipped) are, for the same reason, forced to adapt to the needs of the customers. In this way a beach area is likely to attract the development of harbor and the harbor in turn promotes the development of the beach. We must also notice that no harbor clearly specializes in hosting larger vessels, as even in areas classified "good" or "excellent" bigger boats co-exist in significant percentages with boats under 7 meters.

Plate 2 - Marina and waterfront site living units each with
         mooring (Friuli-V.Giulia)(see Table 3 - Number 5)

Plate 3 - Marina on lagoon like environment (Friuli-
           V.Giulia) (see Table 3 - Number 17)

Conclusion

The location, the structural characteristics and the equipment as well as the quality of the services of marinas are strictly dependent on the kind of customers, and on the degree of development of tourism on the nearby beaches. These factors should be considered along with the physical and socio-economic conditions. Smaller marinas as well as older ones seem to have evolved in a spontaneous way with or without legal permits, in appropriate but peripheral spots for fishermen and enthusiasts and are in some ways related to nautical activities. The more equipped a harbor structure is, and the more recent its construction the more likely it has grown as a result of precise business initiatives.

In order to understand the characteristics of the customers, the analysis suggests, for smaller structures, that one may rely on gravitative models whereas this does not seem to be the case for larger ones, where we find specializations, and strictly functional links to the socio-economic environment in which they are imbedded; in these last ones market forces play a particular role.

It seems that ranking between harbours can be excluded in so far as a prevalence of a certain type not only differentiates the harbours one from the other, but also organizes them into self contained units. Even competition coexists with a certain degree of indifference.

These factors and the mixture of different types of boats create difficulties and shortages in mooring places which may inhibit further diffusion of pleasure boating; an industry interesting not only for socio-economic reasons.

What is needed, therefore, is an integration entailing not so much hierachical links but complemetary relations.

In more general terms, attention should be focused not on the harbor structures themselves and their immediate surroundings but on a circuit which is considerably more vast, which takes into account natural surroundings, infrastructures and socio-economic factors: in a word the area in its entirety.

Notes

1) According to a forecast of the Centro di Calcolo of the University "La Sapienza" of Rome if fiscal policy alters the number of boats in Italy will be about 2,400,000 by 1995 (Ucina-Consornautica, 1988)
2) The ratio of boats to inhabitants is 1 to 114 not counting surfs, inflatable rafts, rowing boats etc. which do not allow for any nautical tourism and leisure. If we add about 30,000 boats of tourists coming from abroad we can evaluate that the potential number of boats in Italian seas in the summer season is somewhere between 520,000 and 550,000.
3) A lack of any landing space or the simplest facilities like equipment for fittings, jetties etc. and the fact that more and more of the beaches are coming under private ownership.

4) In general, being on the river near the outlet (like landings and harbors in the Po delta or the coast between Porto di Lido and Tagliamento) that allows access to the sea, stopping and parking, leaving boats in less dangerous water and above all for leaving small boats near lodging facilities (like camping sites etc.) and seafronts has the disadvantage of sand bars which need to be periodically dredged. The other problem is that it destroys adjacent soil and mud flats when the harbor has to be enlarged (or structures for fittings built). Facilities on the inner borders of lagoons or in related streams are safer and more accessible from inland which is useful for boats pulled by trailer but far from the open sea and present the necessity to overcome long distances to reach open sea and to cope with cumbersome installation work.

5) It is quite difficult to make a distinction between harbor, landing stage, scattered moorings, equipped beaches. Legislation is neither comprehensive nor coherent and so far there is no proper framework thus hindering not only harbors but related industrial sectors. By "harbor" in its wider sense we mean water surface, jetties and installations, sheds, gas stations, safety services, cranes, nautical shops for accessories and tools, snack bars and restaurants etc. all part of the same structure.

6) Out of 500,000 Germans who are members of boating clubs a good 100,000 come to Italy every Summer, most of them bringing their own boats.

7) Depending on the overall facilities and varieties of specialization we gave scores ranging from "inadequate", "adequate", "good" to "excellent".

8) Of the 33 harbors classified as inadequate 24 (73%) have fewer than 150 moorings and 26 (79%) have less than 10,000 m2 of water surface.

9) The clientele was classified as "local" when coming within an hour by car (about 70-80 km). All major towns and numerous small ones are within this limit. National users are those from outlying regions and nearby regions, especially from Lombardia, Emilia-Romagna and Trentino-Alto Adige.

References

BONORA, P.: Produzione e consumo nautico nell'economia del loisir. In: Ucina-Consornautica, La Nautica Italiana (situazione-problemi) 17, I, 33-51, Genova (1984).

BRAMBATI, A.: Studio sedimentologico e marittimo-costiero dei litorali del Friuli-Venezia Giulia, Regione Autonoma Friuli-Venezia Giulia, Direzione Regionale dei Lavori Pubblici, Servizio dell'Idraulica, Trieste (1987).

BRAMBATI, A.: Regime, bilancio sedimentologico e ipotesi di ripascimento dei lidi di Venezia, mimeo (1988).

GOMISCECH, B.: Il turismo nautico nel Friuli-Venezia Giulia, Quad. n.7, Ist. Geogr. Fac. Econ. e Comm. Univ. di Trieste (1987).

RIZZO, G.: Diporto nautico e fascia costiera. In: C.N.R. , Atti del convegno : L'Umanizzazione del mare (Genova 1985) , Roma(1986).

UCINA-CONSORNAUTICA.: La nautica italiana (cifre) 25, Genova 1987

UCINA-CONSORNAUTICA.: Quale nautica per il 1992 (Convegno) 28, Roma 1988

VALUSSI, G.: Lignano Sabbiadoro contributi per una geografia del turismo. Quad. n.2, Ist. Geogr. Fac. Econ. e Comm. di Trieste (1986).

ZUNICA, M.: Le spiagge del Veneto, C.N.R., Padova (1971).

ZUNICA, M.: Italy. In: Bird E.; Schwartz M. (eds.), The World's Coastline, pp.419-423. Van Nostrand Reinhold Company, New York 1985.

Erosional Trends along Cuspate River-Mouths
in the Adriatic Coast

Renske Postma[1]
University of Bologna, Italy

Abstract
The coastlines at the river-mouths of eight selected rivers
along the Adriatic coast of Italy show, in the period
between the end of the nineteenth century and 1935, a
tendency to develop from triangular shaped deltas towards
more straight coastlines. This process is characterized by
erosion as well as by sedimentation. In the subsequent
period until the recent decades, the flattening of the
coastlines has continued, erosion being the predominant
cause. The building up of the deltas in the past as well as
the present-day breakdown, originate from human activities.
Factors important to the formation of the deltas were
deforestation in the mountainous regions and reclamation of
the coastal lowlands. For the present-day erosion, reafforestation, dredging of materials from riverbeds, hydraulic
interventions, urbanization within the coastal zone and
land subsidence, are responsible. At present, since the
economic value of the beaches has increased dramatically
with the rise of tourism, new human activities--at high
expenses--are needed to ensure their protection.

Introduction

The majority of the river deltas along the Adriatic coast
of Italy are threatened by erosion. In this paper, the
processes that are responsible for the formation of the
deltas as well as for the present-day erosion at the river-
mouths, are described. This is done through analysis of
the coastline variations at the mouths of eight selected
rivers, viz. Tagliamento, Piave, Po della Pila, Reno, Fiumi
Uniti, Tronto, Trigno and Fortore (Figure 1). For each
river-mouth, the coastline has been traced for three different years within the last century. As far as possible, the
first year has been chosen at the end of the past century,

[1]Present adress: State University Utrecht, Department
of Physical Geography, Heidelberglaan 2, Postbox 80115,
3508 TC Utrecht, Netherlands.

84

the second one between 1930 and 1940 and the most recent
one within the last two decades.

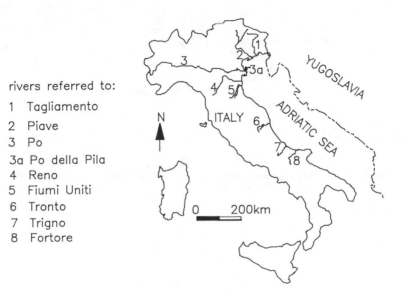

rivers referred to:

1   Tagliamento
2   Piave
3   Po
3a Po della Pila
4   Reno
5   Fiumi Uniti
6   Tronto
7   Trigno
8   Fortore

Figure 1   Location of Selected Rivers

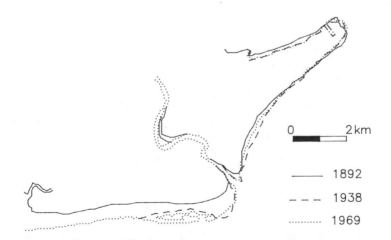

Figure 2   Coastline Variations at the Tagliamento Delta

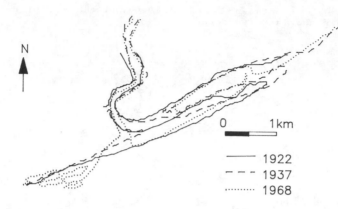

Figure 3   Coastline Variations at the Piave Delta

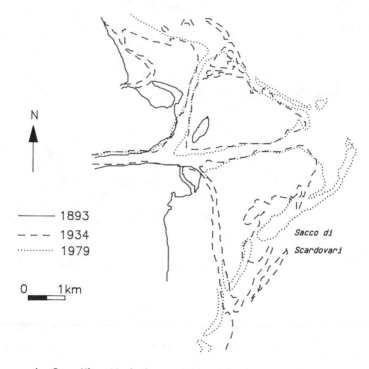

Figure 4   Coastline Variations at the Po della Pila Delta

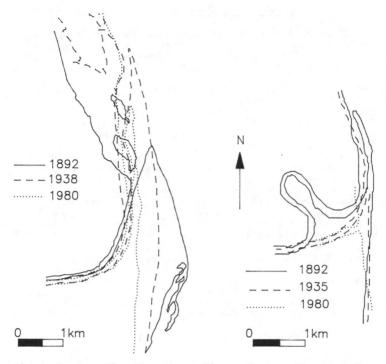

Figure 5 Coastline Variations at the Reno Delta

Figure 6 Coastline Variations at the Fiumi Uniti Delta

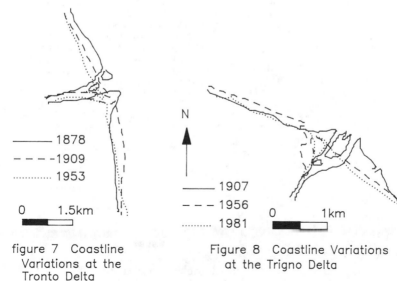

figure 7 Coastline Variations at the Tronto Delta

Figure 8 Coastline Variations at the Trigno Delta

General Trends in Shoreline Developments

In Figures 2 to 9 the coastline variations during the last
100 years at the mouths of eight selected rivers are dis-
played. From this information general trends and characteristic developments can be extracted.

In the period between the end of the past century and approximately 1935, a tendency towards a more straight shoreline can be recognized, in partial combination with advance of the shoreline. The spits of e.g. the Piave and the
Reno are narrowed by erosion from the sea but elongated at
the extremes. The extremes of the spits tend to attach to
the coast, resulting in a smooth and straight shoreline. At
the Tronto, Trigno, and Fortore river-mouths, the cuspate
form of the deltas almost disappears in this period. This
is not just a result of erosion at the river outlet, but
also of advancement of the shoreline at one (Fortore), or
at both sides of the mouth (Tronto and Trigno). The concave
shape of the eastern lobe of the Tagliamento demonstrates a
modest but clear tendency to flatten.

The Po della Pila is an exception during this period. The
shoreline at its delta is not flattened. On the contrary, a
pronounced triangular shape develops, indicating strong
sedimentation at the river-mouth. In the case of the Fiumi
Uniti, a more straight shoreline is developed, however,
without any significant progression of the shoreline.

During the second period, between 1935 and 1970, the flattening of the coastline continues but sedimentation is of
minor importance to this process. Erosion predominates,
occurring severely at the river outlet, whereas at either
side the shoreline is more or less stable as compared to
the 1935 situation. Clear examples of this type of development are the Fortore, Trigno and Tronto. The Reno demonstrates a clear flattening in combination with severe
retreat of the shoreline south of the river-mouth. At the
Tagliamento delta, where the river-mouth has been affected
only slightly by erosion, the general trend can still be
recognized easily. The shoreline of the western lobe strai-
ghtens, but at the eastern lobe only minor changes occur.
The spit of the Piave shrinks at its northern extreme, but
the southern part grows because of the southward displace-
ment of the river-mouth. The spit of the Fiumi Uniti totally disappears and severe erosion affects the river-mouth.

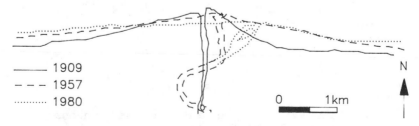

——— 1909
– – – 1957
·········· 1980

                                                      N

0   1km

Figure 9   Coastline Variations at the Fortore Delta

Again, the delta of the Po della Pila demonstrates a development, opposite to that of the other rivers. Its mouth
advances and slight erosion at the southern shore only
pronounces the shape of the delta.

Formation of Cuspate River-Mouths in the Past

Until the beginning of this century, clearly shaped cuspate
forms extended into the sea at the majority of the river-
mouths along the Adriatic coast. Some of these deltas still
exist, e.g. those of the Tagliamento and the Po della Pila.
It has been outlined that during the last 4 decades however, the shorelines at most of the river-mouths straighten
and that the cuspate forms disappear.

For the Po, the location of the river-mouth has been traced
back to 2500 years B.P. (Fabbri, 1985). From this time on,
the Po river has formed a new delta whenever it changed its
course. For the formation of the deltas of the Po and the
deltas of other rivers, huge quantities of sediments must
have been carried to the shore. Two important human activities were responsible for this large supply of sediment:
Deforestation in the mountainous regions and reclamation of
marshlands in coastal areas.

Deforestation
Deforestation started, albeit at a modest scale, at the end
of the Roman Period. In this period, trees were being cut
mainly because of the demand for timber, needed e.g. to
construct boats for the rapidly expanding Roman fleet.
Deforestation was accelerated, when, in the Middle Ages,
people migrated in great numbers from the marshy coastal
zones to the higher and drier mountainous regions. During
this period, large areas of forest were cleared, not just
in order to win timber, but more so to acquire new land for
agriculture and settlement. Between the end of the eigh-
teenth and the middle of the nineteenth century, farming
reached its maximum extent and large areas on the Italian
peninsula were deforestated (Parea, in Bird and Fabbri,
1983).

Reclamation
Up to the beginning of this century, the founding of settlements in the coastal zone was unattractive. In the extensive marshlands, especially in the surroundings of major
rivers, malaria was widespread and, in the Middle Ages,
piracy was a realistic threat. At the end of the past
century, reclamation of the marshlands began. In the inter-
war years, and especially under Mussolini in the twenties,
large reclamation schemes were initiated to meet the need
for agricultural land and to suppress malaria.

Reclaimed land is drained by canals, that transport the
excess water into the nearby river or directly into the
sea. Sediments are transported by the water and dumped at

the river-mouth. It is assumed that this process has contributed considerably to the formation of riverdeltas in
the Adriatic coast.

An example is the reclamation process in the Tronto river
delta (Figure 10). In 1878 hardly any agricultural activity
existed in the Tronto delta. In 1909, the greater part of
the delta was reclaimed and especially south of the river-
mouth, many canals were connected directly to the sea. From
Figure 7, it can be seen that especially in this zone, the
shoreline advanced considerably between 1878 and 1909.

The delta of the Po della Pila has been expanding until
recently. This continued expansion can partly be explained
by the reclamation schemes in the Po delta, which started
in 1890 and were completed only in the 1960's (Fabbri,
1985). Another cause for the expansion is the reorgani-
zation of the dyke system in the Po delta following two
extraordinary floods in 1872 and 1879. Henceforth, the
lateral discharge of water containing suspended sediments,
diminished and consequently more material was deposited at
the river-mouth (Visentini and Borghi, 1938).

Processes that Cause Erosion at River-Mouths

In the period between 1935 and 1970, erosion predominates
at most of the river-mouths. While the extreme sedimentation in the period until the beginning of this century was
caused by an increase of the sediment discharge of the

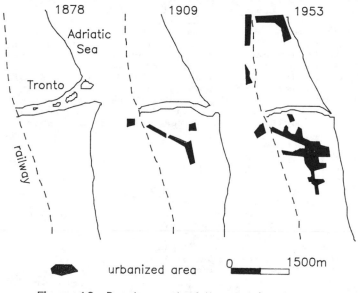

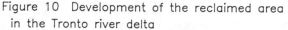

Figure 10 Development of the reclaimed area
in the Tronto river delta

rivers, symmetrically the erosion in the present century
can be related to a decrease in the discharge. A 20-50%
decrease in the mean annually transported quantity of
alluvial silt between 1952 and 1971 in rivers discharging
into the Adriatic Sea, was reported by Vittorini (1980). In
the cases of the Po and the Fortore, this diminution was
found only from 1962 onward. Apart from this, in some
regions subsidence of the land is leading to a retreat of
the coastline. The relative importance of eustatic sea
level rise, is still unclear.

Three processes that reduce discharge of sediment through
rivers are described below: a)reafforestation in moutainous
regions; b)dredging of gravel and sand from riverbeds;
c)hydraulic interventions in watersheds. Two more processes
that cause coastal erosion--urbanization within the coastal
zone and subsidence--are discussed.

Reafforestation

Reafforestation is carried out especially in mountainous
areas for reasons of soil protection. Since the extended
reclamation schemes in the coastal zone have been completed, most of the agricultural land in the mountains is
abandoned and is subjected to reafforestation. Between 1950
and 1970, the woodland area in Italy increased by 600,000
hectares as a result of reafforestation (Vittorini, 1980).
Of all watersheds belonging to rivers that flow into the
Adriatic Sea, those in the Abruzzo region have been reafforestated most extensively. An example is the watershed of
the Fortore, where numerous new forests of varying size
have been planted (Figure 11). In the watersheds of Tagliamento and Piave, reafforestation has affected a much smaller area, although all agricultural and zootechnical activity has been abandoned. Only few areas are planted in the
lower mountains and very few in the higher mountains. Yet,
reafforestation in this region is badly needed to restore
the deteriorated hydro-geological situation.

Dredging

Gravel and sand are being dredged from almost all the
principal riverbeds. After World War II, the demand for
sand and gravel, needed to construct roads and buildings,
increased enormously. On a smaller scale, bed materials are
being extracted by olive squeezing plants. These are widespread along e.g. the Tronto. Information on the quantity
of bed material that is extracted, however, is very scarce.
Extraction is limited by law, but effective control is
lacking. The officially registered amounts of extracted
bed materials do not provide a reliable view of the extent
of this activity. That amounts are sizeable, is shown in a
study on the extraction of bed material from four rivers in
the Emilia-Romagna region, viz. Savio, Uso, Marecchia and
Conca (Antoniazzi, 1976). It has been estimated that,
between 1957 and 1972, a total amount of 9,2 million cubic
metres of bed material was extracted from these rivers.
Pellegrini (in Consiglio Nazionale delle Ricerche, 1978)
found that the riverbed of the Reno in its initial course,

was lowered by 2 metres over a distance of 5 kilometres in
the period 1928-1970 as a result of dredging activities.

Hydraulic interventions
During this century, many artificial lakes have been constructed, mainly in mountainous regions. The stored water
is being used for the generation of hydro-electrical energy
or for irrigation purposes.

Table 1   STORAGE CAPACITY OF ARTIFICIAL LAKES IN SOME
          ITALIAN RIVERS

RIVERCOURSE	NUMBER OF LAKES	USE*	TOT. CAPACITY
			$(*10^6 \ m^3)$
Tagliamento	4	E	73.4
Piave	12	E,I	316.05
Tronto	3	E	111.5
Fortore	1		333.0

* E= hydro-electrical
   I= irrigation

Source: Ministero dell'Agricoltura e delle Foreste, 1976.

The storage of water and sediment in artificial lakes, dis-
rupts the normal downstream sediment transport. The river
bed will have to adapt its profile to the new situation,
when a reservoir is put into use. Downstream profile changes depend on the relative reductions of the water and
sediment discharges, and on the initial sedimentology of
the river. The percentage of the sediment discharge trapped
in a reservoir depends on the granulometrical composition
of the sediment load. The stored percentage is larger in
rivers with a predominance of bed-load than it is in the
case of a mainly suspended load. If the trapping efficiency
is high, degradation of the riverbed may occur downstream
of the reservoir. If the bed material is a sand-gravel
mixture and supposing the natural discharge peaks are not
fully suppressed, degradation continues until only the
coarser bed sediments--which cannot be moved--are left. It
is commonly assumed that artificial lakes result in a
decrease of the sediment transport towards the river-mouth.
For the rivers described in this paper, data on changes in
sediment transport after the construction of artificial
lakes, are not available. However, in the Bradano river, in
the Basilicata region, a clear decrease in the annually
transported alluvial silt from 2,304,000 tons before the
construction of the San Giuliano dam to 176,000 tons after-
wards, has been measured (Vittorini, 1980). Table 1 indicates the total capacity of the principal artificial lakes
in selected watersheds. Especially in the Piave and the
Fortore watersheds, the artificial lakes intercept a large

amount of water. This must have resulted in a substancial decrease in the sediment load in the terminal courses of these rivers.

Since ancient times, rivers have been used to adapt the coastal marshlands in Italy to agricultural puposes. An area of marshland would be enclosed by dykes and the course of a nearby river would be guided through it. After some time, the river would have deposited so much sediment that the level of the land would have been increased to enable cultivation. Subsequently, a new area would be enclosed. This activity has deprived the river-mouth of e.g. the Fiumi Uniti from a large part of the sediment supply. This river has been used to raise extensive areas in the surroundings of Ravenna.

Revetments along river channels, stabilizing the course of a river and preventing lateral erosion, often result in a decrease of the sediment discharge. Numerous revetments

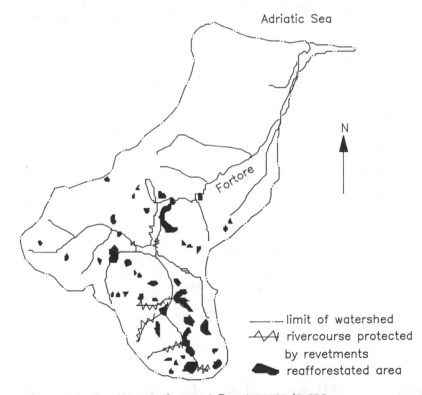

Adriatic Sea

N

Fortore

———— limit of watershed
∿∿ rivercourse protected
by revetments
reafforestated area

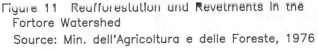

Figure 11   Reafforestation and Revetments in the Fortore Watershed
Source: Min. dell'Agricoltura e delle Foreste, 1976

have been constructed in the upper portions of most of the
watersheds. Figure 11 shows the extent of revetments in the
watersheds of the Fortore.

Urbanization within the coastal zone
With the growth of beach oriented tourism in the 1950s,
urbanized areas within the coastal zone expanded explosive-
ly. This is shown in Figure 12 and 13, which illustrate the
development of urbanized areas in the deltas of the Piave
and the Tagliamento. Until recently, dune areas and the
still marshy river deltas were considered useless for
purposes of urbanization and were sold at low prices. Large
entrepreneurs bought vast areas along the coast and furnis-
hed these for use by the lucrative tourist industry, con-
structing roads and condominiums. Houses were built as
close as possible to the sea, on flattened dunes or even on
the beach. Thus, dunes were removed from the coastal system. Since, in some regions, dunes can no longer supply
any sand to the system, part of the beach material irrever-
sibly disappears into sea during storms. This process
results in erosion until a new equilibrium has been established.

Coastal Subsidence
The influence of subsidence differs strongly between regions. For the Emilia-Romagna region, coastal subsidence has
been pointed out as the most important sediment sink (Til-
man, 1985). For Ravenna it has been estimated that subsidence of isostatic origin has caused a lowering of the land
at a mean velocity of 0.65-1.3 mm/annum since the last
glaciation. The relative rise of the sea-level in this
region has been 2-3 mm/annum during the last 2000 years
(Consiglio Nazionale delle Ricerche, 1979). The extraction
of water and gas from the soil has noticeably increased
the velocity of coastal subsidence: It has been estimated
that since 1950, the velocity of coastal subsidence in the
surroundings of Ravenna has been 3.67 mm/annum (Paskoff,
1985).

Heavy pumping of ground water in newly developed areas and
compaction of sediments after reclamation have caused
increased subsidence in the Po delta (Fabbri, 1985). This
has resulted in a recession of the coastline at e.g. the
Sacca di Scardovari (Figure 4). Recently, this bay has been
embanked and it is now protected by seawalls.

Conclusions

Along the Adriatic coast of Italy, there is a development
towards a more straight shoreline, implying the smoothing
of pronounced coastal forms such as triangular river deltas. This trend is characterized by erosion at river-mouths
and sedimentation on both sides. The net change of the
overall beach-volume along the Adriatic coast has never
been determined and it may even be positive. However,
locally, erosion can be a serious problem: Erosion at one

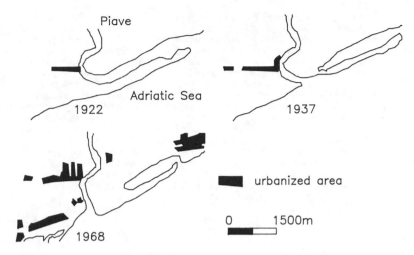

Piave

Adriatic Sea

1922

1937

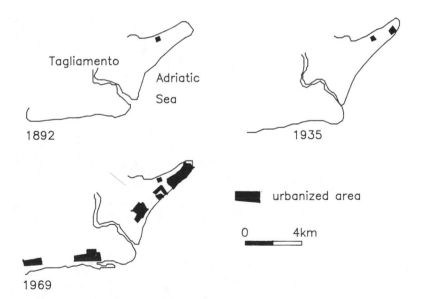

urbanized area

0   1500m

1968

Figure 12   Development of the Urbanized Area
in the Piave River Delta

Tagliamento

Adriatic

Sea

1892

1935

urbanized area

0   4km

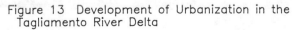

1969

Figure 13   Development of Urbanization in the
Tagliamento River Delta

place cannot be compensated by sedimentation at another
place. With the rise of tourism, the economic value of
coastal areas has increased enormously and large investments have been made and will have to be made, to protect
the shore where necessary. In some cases, the protection
works have had very positive results as far as the increase
of the beach area is concerned. For example, the shoreline
between Rimini and Cattolica has advanced noticeably,
although the endless series of detached breakwaters and
groynes has reduced its aesthetic value. In other places,
however, the defence works deteriorate the situation by
displacing the erosive activity downdrift. Since the advance of the shoreline in the past and its recession in the
present century both resulted from human activities, it is
likely that the protection of the coastal zone will have to
be the result of new, carefully planned, human intervention.

REFERENCES

ANTONIAZZI, A. (1976) L'erosione marina nel litorale fra
Cervia e Pesaro, pp 161, Forli.

BIRD, E.C.F. and P.FABBRI (Eds) (1983) Coastal problems in
the Mediterranean Sea, Proc. of a Symposium of the International Geograghical Union, Comm. on the Coastal
Environment, Venice.

MINISTERO DELL'AGRICOLTURA E DELLE FORESTE (1976), Carta
della Montagna. Direzione generale per l'economia montana e
per le foreste.

CONSIGLIO NAZIONALE DELLE RICERCHE (1979) Le spiagge di
Romagna: Uno spazio da proteggere, Progette Finalizzato
Conservazione del suolo, quaderno 1, Bologna.

FABBRI, P. (1985) Coastline variations in the Po delta
since 2500 B.P., Z. Geomorph. N.F., Suppl.-Bd 57, 155-167,
Dez. 1985.

PASKOFF, R. (1985) L'erosione delle spiagge: L'originalita
del Mediterraneo, In:Coastal Planning: Realities and Perspectives, International Seminar of the International
Geograghical Union, Genova, 1985.

TILMANS, W.M.K., G. BAARSE, H.A. VAN PAGEE, D. FONTANA (-
1985) Coastal zone management in Emilia-Romagna, Italy,
In:Proc. of the Symp. on the Coastal Zone '85.

VISENTINO, M. and G. BORGHI (1938) Ricerche sulle varia-
zioni delle spiagge italiane, Vol VII:Le spiagge padane.
Con. Naz. delle Ricerche, Istituto di Geografia, Bologna.

VITTORINI, S. (1980) Italian coasts and their recent changes, In: Italy, a geographical survey, Publ. for the 24th
International Geographical Congress, Tokyo, 1980.

Coastal zoning and vulnerability: application to the Middle Adriatic (Italy)

Renzo Dal Cin* and Umberto Simeoni*

Abstract

A method is proposed to obtain coastal zoning and to evaluate the vulnerability of the coastal strip behind the beach. The method was applied to the beaches of northern Marches (Middle Adriatic - Italy.

The following procedure was used for coastal zoning: the coast between Pesaro and Ancona (62 km) was divided into 22 stretches, each 2-3 km long. For each segment, 18 variables were quantified because of their importance in characterizing the coast and in the understanding of its evolution. The variables are grouped as follows: hydrodynamic (3 variables), evolutive (4), sedimentological (3), morphological (6) and anthropic (2)

In order to group the segments according to the similarity of the 18 variables, Q mode factor analysis and cluster analysis were employed. As a result, three principal homogeneous groups emerged which include 17 of the 22 segments. The remaining five coastal stretches are classified in intermediate positions between the three principal groups.

In order to evaluate coastal vulnerability, the following procedure was used. The subject of the vulnerability study is the onshore coastal strip extending landward from the beach. This zone, either urbanized or under cultivation, can be damaged during severe storms or by exceptionally high water. Its principal defense from natural hazards is represented by certain morphological elements of emerged and submerged beaches and by maritime structures.

Factor analysis has shown that the coastal stretches with characteristics providing safety (protective structures; wide and high, stable beaches; gently sloping submerged beaches with an abundance of bars; low energy flux of waves) are represented by factors I and III . The segments which are characterized by conditions of risk (unprotected, low and narrow, retreating beaches; steep, nearshore beds with few or no bars; high energy flux) are represented by factor II. For each segment, the vulnerability of the

---

* Dipartimento di Scienze Geologiche e Paleontologiche, Università, 44100 Ferrara (Italy)

coastal strip extending landward from the beach was calculated by determining the percentage of factor II with respect to the sum of factors I and III .

Introduction

The method proposed here for identifying and grouping similar coastal segments and for evaluating the vulnerability of the onshore coastal strip behind the beach areas was applied to the coast between Pesaro and Ancona (Middle Adriatic - Italy) (fig. 1). This is a 62 km beach which constitutes a physiographic unit, lying between two rocky promontories   (fig. 2). This natural unit is divided into artificial sub-units delimited by the ports of Pesaro, Fano and Senigallia.

Figure 1. Location of coast.

The variations of the shoreline (Dal Cin et al., 1984) were slight until the 1940's .   During   the   last   30-40   years,   coastal retreats have been greatly accentuated, particularly at the mounts of the Metauro, Cesano and Esino Rivers (fig. 2). Erosion was caused primarily by the reduced fluvial sediment discharge. Over the years, various kinds of defense structures have been built in an effort to counteract erosion; at present, about 54 % of the coast is protected (fig. 2).

In the sampled area, sand beaches prevail (45 %) as compared to gravel (35 %) and mixed (20 %). The longshore drift moves toward the   northwest,   whereas   the   dispersion   of   suspended   fluvial sediments (< 0.06 mm) is, in general, out to sea or to the northwest (fig. 2).

A sedimentological study (Dal Cin and Simeoni, 1987), conducted along the emerged beaches and sea beds to a depth of -12 m , indicates the following: scarcity of mud fractions to a depth of   8-10

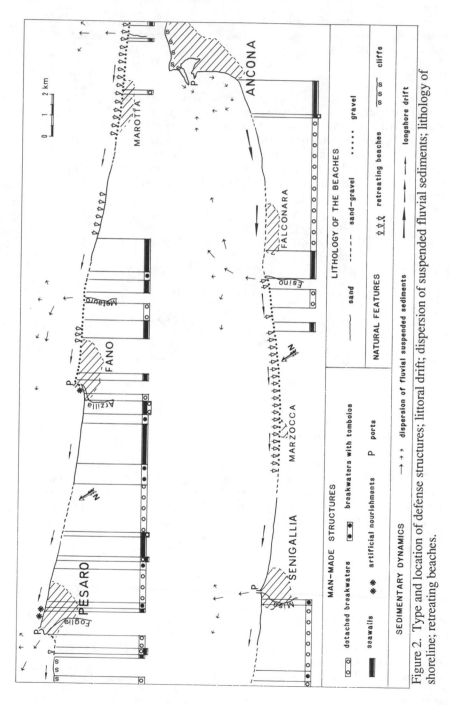

Figure 2. Type and location of defense structures; littoral drift; dispersion of suspended fluvial sediments; lithology of shoreline; retreating beaches.

m ; the presence of slightly mobile residual sediments in a belt lying between -3 and -9 m; elevated mobility of sediments between 0 and -3 m ; extremely scarce fluvial discharge of sands and gravels ; considerable sedimentological homogeneity of the sea bottoms to a depth of 10 m ; prevalence of fine and very fine sands between 0 and -10 m ; sedimentological and morphological processes of the sea beds controlled primarily by wave action.

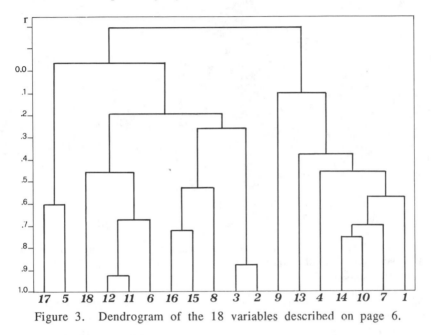

Figure 3.   Dendrogram of the 18 variables described on page 6.

Coastal zoning

Method

The possibility of identifying and grouping similar coastal stretches on the basis of their physical environmental characteristics represents an important tool for the effective management of the coast and for the formulation of reliable predictions regarding its evolution.

The more numerous the variables affecting the coast taken into consideration and the more correct then quantification, the more complete, objective and statistically correct will be the resulting zoning.

This attempt to group similar coastal stretches required the preliminary solution of three principal methodological problems : 1) how to subdivide the coast in question and into how many segments; 2) which mathematical-statistic methods to apply for grouping and for classifying hierarchically the selected coastal stretches; 3) among the various factors that characterize the coast, which to choose and how to quantify them.

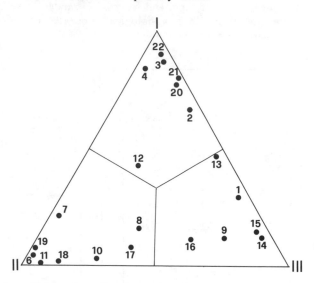

Figure 4. Triangular diagram of the "weight" of the individual coastal segments on the three factors. For the location of each segment see fig.6.

With respect to the first point, the coast lying between Pesaro and Ancona was divided into 22 segments, each of 2 to 3 km in length. This length did not seem so great as to include extremely diverse situations, nor so small as to give undue importance to local situations. Furthermore, the number of stretches was conditioned by the number of points in which several important variables were quantified. An exemple are the variables of energy flux and longshore drift, which were quantified in 22 stations.

The limits between adjacent stretches often correspond to relevant morphological or man-made features, as river outlets, ports, defense structures.

For each of the 22 segments, 18 variables were quantified which were considered important to characterize the coastal situation or to control its evolution. Regarding the criteria employed in the choice of variables and their quantification, the reader is referred to Dal Cin and Simeoni (1987) and Dal Cin (1989).

The variables taken into consideration are hydrodynamic and energetic (3 variables), evolutive (4), sedimentological (3), morphological (6) and man-made (2).

Hydrodynamic and energetic variables (Aquater, 1982, 1984):   1-mean energy flux (kw/m) ;   2- global longshore transport (m³/year);   3- littoral drift (m³/year).

Variables regarding shoreline evolution :   4- average shoreline advancement from 1892 to 1948 (m/year) ;   5- average shoreline retreat from 1892 to 1948 (m/year) ;   6- average shoreline advancement from 1948 to 1987 (m/year) ;   7- average shoreline retreat from 1948 to 1987 (m/year) .

Sedimentological variables :   8- percentage of sand on the emerged beach ;   9- mean size of the sea bed between depths 0 and -3 m (in mm) ;   10- percentage of decrease, with reference to the period before 1960, of the bedload discharge of the major rivers.

Morphological variables :   11- volume of the emerged beach ; 12- width of the emerged beach ;   13- height of the emerged beach ;   14- slope of the emerged beach ;   15- width of the strip between 0 and -3 m ;   16- presence of bars on the bottom.

Man-made variables :   17- defense structures and ports ;   18-percentage of urbanized territory onshore in the first 200 m behind the beach.

In order to obtain the coastal zoning based on the variables listed above, it was decided to employ Q mode factor analysis and cluster analysis. These techniques have provided good results in analogous research dealing with other Adriatic coasts (Dal Cin and Simeoni, 1987, 1989; Dal Cin, 1989). Multivariate analysis was also applied successfully by Blanc (1980) and Blanc and Froget (1979) in the dynamic sedimentary analysis of the coasts of Provence (France).

The data obtained by the quantification of the 18 variables were subsequently normalized and homogenized according to the procedures reported in Dal Cin and Simeoni (1987).

Results

Before determining the coastal zoning, relationships and interactions between the 18 variables were analyzed by means of R-mode factor and cluster analyses. The dendrogram in fig. 3 is the result of the cluster analysis.

Positive correlations are evident between the retreat of the coast, decrease of fluvial sediment discharge, energy flux and slope of the beach. Bars characterize gently sloping sea beds with sandy beaches. Onshore urbanization has developed primarily along wide, high volume beaches which are either in a stage of advancement or in equilibrium. The mean grain size between 0 and -3 m does not show significant variations; it is essentially conditioned by the waves. Given their limited sediment discharge, the rivers do not influence the mean size, not even immediately nearshore, nor when the supply consists of gravel.

The grouping of the 22 coastal segments according to the similarity of the 18 variables was obtained, as stated above, by using Q mode factor analysis and cluster analysis. Factor analysis shows that three factors are sufficient to account for 84 % of the total variance. The use of four factors increases the variance by only 4 % ; the interpretation. however. becomes much more complex.

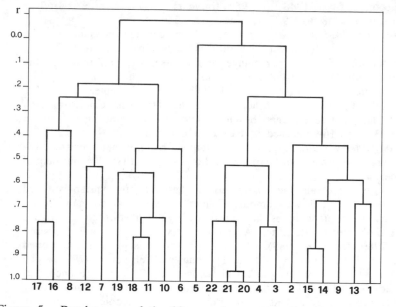

Figure 5.   Dendrogram of the 22 coastal segments. For the location of each segment see fig.6.

The communality is almost always higher than 0.8 , but in all cases greater than 0.7 . Only segment five (Fano beach) has a very low communality (0.54), and therefore connot be adequately represented by only three factors. As a result, segment five was not classified.

The results of the factor analysis are presented in fig. 4. This was obtained by normalizing the "weighting" of each segment on the three factors.

Factor I   (27.9 % of the variance) primarily includes segments 22-3-4-21-20 and, subordinately, segment 2 .

Factor II   (29.0 % of the variance) prevalently associates segments 6-11-19-18 and, to a lesser degree, segments 7 and 10.

Factor III   (27.2 % of the variance) principally groups segments 14-15 and, secondarily, segments 1 and 9.

Other segments belong to two factors contemporaneously: primarily segments 13 (factors I-III) and, to a lesser degree, segments 17-8-16 (factors II-III) and segment 12 (factors I-II).

In order to quantify the similarity of the various coastal stretches and establish the hierarchical succession of the match-ups, cluster analysis was employed using the matrix of correlation coefficients. The dendrogram in fig. 5 summarizes the results of the analysis.

The groupings with the highest similarities (lying between 0.96 and 0.74) are formed by the following segments : 20-21-22, 14-15, 10-11-18, 3-4, 16-17. Almost all the strongest match-ups, therefore, are formed by adjacent segments : consequently, in a limited area, the coastal characteristics often vary only slightly and with continuity.

In the match-ups listed above, no segment is divided from another by the mouth of a river or by a port; in no match-up is one segment protected and another not. One may deduce therefore, that the river mouths and maritime structures are among the most

By synthesizing the results of factor and cluster analyses, and by taking into consideration the correlations between the variables, the 22 coastal segments fall into three fundamental groups A-B-C and three secondary groups BC-AC-AB (fig. 6).

Group A - Includes segments 22-3-4-21-20-2 ; this group represents the coastal area between Pesaro and Fano and between Falconara and Ancona (fig. 6). These coastal stretches have the following characteristics: all are protected by massive defense structures (mainly seawalls and detached breakwaters); all were in a retreating phase prior to the 1950's; normally, they present very few bars; in some cases, they are intensively urbanized onshore.

Group B - Represented by segments 6-11-19-18-7-10, which are located at or near the mouths of the Metauro, Cesano and Esino Rivers (fig. 6), the principal rivers found in the area studied. These coastal stretches present the following characteristics: they are at present in accentuated retreat whereas, prior to 1948 , they were prograding; they are strongly influenced by decreased fluvial sediment discharge; they are affected by a considerable energy flux; they present rather narrow, very steep gravel beaches which, in some cases, have a high maximun elevation; the beds between 0 an -3 m are very steep and either have very few bars or none at all. Certain segments (6-7-19) are either partially or completely protected.

Group C - Formed by segments 14-15-9-1 (fig. 6). These stretches may be described as follows: they are not protected (except segment 1 which is partially protected); the coast is in a stage of substantial equilibrium; the emerged beaches are very wide and sandy, with high volume, high maximum elevation and gentle sloping; these segments are influenced by a low energy flux; the beds between 0 and -3 m are gently sloping and rich in bars; in some cases onshore urbanization is intensive.

The segments which belong to groups *BC* , *AB* and *AC* present intermediate characteristics between those of groups *A-B-C* .

Group BC   -   Includes segments 8-17-16 . These are narrow, partially gravel, retreating beaches which are not protected, and which have a low energy flux, gently sloping bottoms and only slight onshore urbanization.

Group AB   -   Only segment 12 belongs to this group. Its beaches are characterized by detached breakwaters; the beaches are steep and narrow, partially gravel, lacking in bars and slightly urbanized. Essentially, this segment presents the typical traits of beaches near river mouths (group *A*) but, in reality, it is protected.

Group AC   -   Represented by segment 13 . This is a stretch with detached seawalls, very wide, gently sloping, sandy beaches with onshore urbanization; the sea beds are slightly inclined, but have only a few bars.

Evaluation of coastal vulnerability

Vulnerability represents an indispensable factor in calculating coastal risk. Its definition and quantification in a coastal environment are neither simple nor without subjective elements. It is important to define the subject of vulnerability. Along a coast, the vulnerable subject could be a beach. In that case, the vulnerability could be evaluated by determining, for example, the capacity of the beach to resist the erosive processes which tend to destroy it. In this study, the subject of vulnerability is the onshore coastal zone located behind the beach and extending landward for a certain number of meters. This strip of land has a high economic and environmental value because it is often urbanized or under cultivation or because it is the location of important historical and cultural elements.

This belt, whose width may very from tens of meters to several hundred meters, can be damaged or even destroyed by severe storms, particularly when these are combined with exceptionally high tides. The primary defense of this area from natural hazard is represented by the emerged beach, the morphology of the inshore beds and by man-made defense structures. Therefore, the strip behind the beach is the subject of vulnerability and the beach is the element of defense from natural hazard.

It is obvious, for example, that a very wide beach with a high maximum elevation will provide considerable protection for the area behind it, all other conditions being equal; the opposite will be true for a low, narrow beach.

Based on these considerations, several of the 18 variables quantified above were taken as factors that may cause an increase or decrease in the protective function of the beach and, consequently, may cause an increase or decrease in the vulnerability of the strip behind the beach.

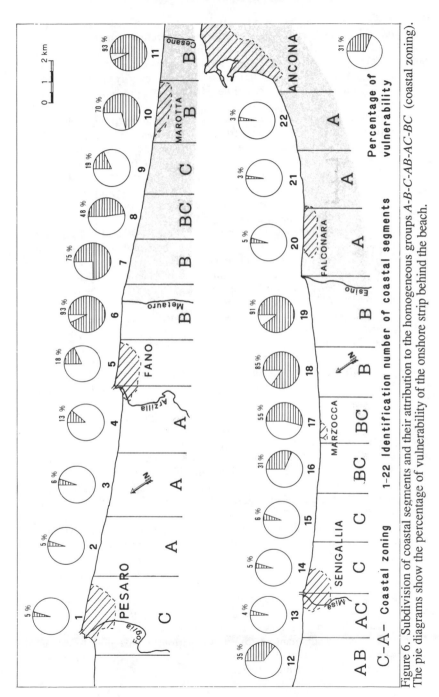

Figure 6. Subdivision of coastal segments and their attribution to the homogeneous groups *A-B-C-AB-AC-BC* (coastal zoning). The pie diagrams show the percentage of vulnerability of the onshore strip behind the beach.

High values of width, height and volume of the beach are favourable, "natural" elements providing protection for the backing area. Gently sloping beds from 0 to -3 meters which are rich in sand bars are also safety factors because they favour the dissipation of wave energy. Other positive elements are low energy flux and the tendency of the beaches to be either in a phase of equilibrium or advancement.

Q-mode factor analysis has shown (see preceding paragraph) that high values of the above-mentioned variables characterize the coastal segments grouped in factor III . More specifically, the greater the "weight" of a segment on factor III, the higher the values of these variables in that segment. At the first level of approximation, we can therefore consider the "weight" on factor III as the quantification of the natural protection that each single segment offers the belt behind the beach.

Defense structures, particularly seawalls and detached breakwaters, are another important element causing a decrease in vulnerability. Factor analysis clearly indicates that the better a beach is defended, the greater its incidence on factor I . Therefore, this factor quantifies the protection of the onshore strip behind the beach as a result of human intervention.

Vice versa, there are negative elements for safety: low volume, narrow, low beaches; very steep inshore beds with absence or scarcity of bars; absence of defense structures; retreating tendency of beaches; high energy flux. These elements are common to the coastal segments with a high factor II incidence. Therefore, "weight" on this fact can quantify the elements that generate coastal vulnerability.

In conclusion, factors I and III quantify elements that provide safety: factor I due to natural causes, factor III as a result of human intervention. By summing the two factors, we obtain total safety. Factor II, instead, quantifies the degree of insecurity and therefore the vulnerability of the strip behind the beach. For each coastal segment, the vulnerability of this area can be calculated by determining the percentage of factor II with respect to the sum of factors I and III.

Fig. 6 presents pie diagrams showing the degree of vulnerability of the coast in question. The most vulnerable stretches are those near or corresponding to the mouths of major rivers. Several of these beaches are either partially or totally protected by man-made structures (segments 6-7-19). In these cases, their high vulnerability must be understood in this sense: the defense structures, located along retreating coasts, in bottoms which are very steep and lacking in bars and subject to a strong energy flux, will be more easily dismantled by wave action. Consequently, they will require more careful control and more frequent repair, resulting, therefore in greater costs.

The least vulnerable stretches are those which are protected or located upstream with respect to the most important ports (Pesaro, Senigallia). Segment 5 (Fano), in spite of the fact that its classification is problematic due to low communality, belongs to this category.

Conclusions

The application of the methods described above made it possible to objectively group similar coastal stretches on the basis of their physical and man-made characteristics. The ability to identify pairs or groups of homogeneous coastal segments represents an important tool for the effective management of the coast and for the As a result, if a given intervention in a coastal segment (for example, construction or modification of defense structures and ports, artificial nourishment, etc.) has caused certain effects, this study will allow us to determine in which other segments the same intervention will have similar effects.

Analogous considerations can be made for any future studies in sample areas: the choice of the area and the extrapolation of the data obtained in other similar coastal areas will be facilitated by coastal zoning.

The possibility of evaluating the vulnerability of the strip behind the beach is indispensable for quantifying coastal risk. The method presented in this study clearly presents certain limitations: no doubt, it can be improved by quantifying other variables which influence the coast and by applying other, more sophisticated mathematical procedures. In addition, an evaluation must be made regarding the problem of an effective complete adaptability of this method to other situations which are significantly different from those along the Adriatic coast.

Among the advantages of the method proposed here, there is an adequate simplicity as well as the possibility of utilizing the coastal zoning data without further elaboration.

References

Aquater: Regione Marche. Studio generale per la difesa delle coste: prima fase. Vol. 1, Relazione generale ; Vol. 2, Rapporti di settore (1982).

Aquater: Regione Marche. Studio generale per la difesa delle coste: seconda fase. Analisi del regime del trasporto litoraneo e bilancio dei sedimenti. Snamprogetti (1984).

Blanc, J.J.: Sedimentologie dynamique des plages de Provence. Methodologie et études d'impact. Cent. Nat. pou l'exploitation des oceans, Marseille (1980).

Blanc, J.J.; Froget, C.H. : Présentation d'une mèthode d'analyse
    sèdimentaire dynamique appliquée aux plages. L'exemple du
    littoral de la Camargue. Bull. du Bureau de Rech. Geol. et Min.,
    2, pp. 91-102 (1979).
Dal Cin, R.: I litorali fra S. Bendetto del Tronto e Ortona (Medio
    Adriatico): sedimenti, degrado ambientale, zonazione costiera,
    possibili strategie d'intervento. Boll. Soc. Geol. It., in print
    (1989).
Dal Cin, R.; Pedone, F.; Simeoni, U.: Morphological evolution and
    sediment distribution on the coasts of the Marches (Central
    Adriatic, Italy). Soc. Hydrotec. de France, "L'hydraulique et la
    maitrise du littoral", Marseille (1984).
Dal Cin, R.; Simeoni, U.: Analisi ambientale quantitativa dei litorali
    marchigiani fra Gabicce e Ancona. Livello del rischio naturale e
    del degrado. Distribuzione dei sedimenti e loro possibile
    impiego per ripascimenti artificiali. Boll. Soc. Geol. It., 106, pp.
    377-423 (1987).
Dal Cin, R.; Simeoni, U.: L'analisi multivariata applicata alla
    caratterizzazione ambientale dei litorali abruzzesi compresi fra
    il Tronto e Francavilla Boll. Soc. Geol. It., in print (1989).

The Use of the Sea for Leisure Activities: the case of the Ligurian Sea

Giovanni Ridolfi *

Abstract

The Ligurian Sea, extending within the straight lines which reach from Cape Corso (Island of Corsica) westwards to the area of the Italian-French frontier and eastwards to the Promontory of Piombino (along the 43rd parallel), washes against just under 500 km of coastlands, two-thirds of which are in the region of Liguria and one-third in Tuscany.

Apart from a few short tracts, these coastal areas have considerable attraction for humans, resulting in intense urban and industrial development, port and harbour facilities, resorts for tourism and leisure activities. These latter boast early origins and have developed a highly mature organisational and productive level, thus becoming essential to the economy of the entire coastal region.

The fulcrum of leisure activities of this coastal zone is the sea: it is the determining factor for the climate, an important element of the landscape, an attraction for health-giving and pleasure-seeking leisure and a ground for many kinds of sporting activities. But the co-existence of leisure with the other numerous uses of the Ligurian Sea is not easy; on the contrary, it is sometimes difficult and almost impossible.

The lack, up to the present, of efficient operative means and of a wise management of the coastal zone has often encouraged the gradual transformation of the original spontaneous development into accentuated speculative processes. Many precious values of the environment have been spoiled and consequently a great deal of the socio-cultural values of local populations has diminished.

As a consequence, in comparison with other Italian seas, the Ligurian Sea presents the peculiarity of concentrating the most urgent and compelling factors concerned with the traditional and new uses of the littoral waters. At present there seem to be perspectives of a more responsible protection and evaluation of the available natural and human resources to the general advantage of communities living along the coast and of those who stay there temporarily.

----

* G. Ridolfi, Istituto di Scienze Geografiche, Lungoparco Gropallo 3, 16122 Genova, Italia

A coast for tourism and leisure.

Tourism is in continuous and rapid evolution throughout the world, especially where favourable natural conditions tie up with human incentives: this is also the case of the Ligurian Sea.

Underlying the expansion of tourism there is, above all, the fact of a general increase in national income and its wider distribution at different social levels. Added to this, there is a great deal more free time available because of the shrinking of working time and easy and convenient mobility made possible by the improved public and private transport facilities.

Finally, but not least important, there is the quantitative and qualitative development that tourism can activate: highly sophisticated in regions with long-standing touristic traditions; more modern and functional in recently developed areas.

Along with economic factors, which offer the possibility of mobility, there are the social ones which encourage the necessity of total or partial commitment for the holiday period to touristic activities (those include at least one night away from home and therefore involving a number of productive and consumer activities, mainly directed at the visiting tourist, that is the visitor from a distance away) and, for leisure time, to recreational activities (those designed for entertainment and relaxation, which are intended not only for the visitor but also for the local population, that is for those who live nearby).

Stresses deriving from activities in the new forms of social life produced by extensive urbanisation increasingly highlight the individual's need for relief from everyday routine. Sociological and psychological needs, induced by the spread of information and education stimulate participation in events (sporting, cultural, social) and visits to places (traditional, exotic, fashionable) either in the immediate neighbourhood or at some distance away. Often these activities are based on simply imitative impulses.

From this potential demand, within reach of the entire local population, arises the effective demand, coming from non residents who are able to respond to the touristic-leisure offer according to the free time they have, as well as their economic possibilities.

These requirements, normally related to individual or families ways of life, range from the simplest forms of mass tourism to exclusive and élitest forms.

Each region, according to its environmental characteristics (the area's physical connotations, historic, artistic resources, the built-up districts, the local socio-cultural values), accessibility and accomodation capacities provides the type of recreation most consistent with its political, economic and territorial objectives.

In the context of a systemic view of the region, leisure functions are an element of internal territorial importance - for the whole of the structure involved in

tourism supply and for the entire local population concerned
with recreation demand - and, at the same time, a necessary
external opening towards the ever widening horizons of
tourism demand.
       The   most   advantageous   touristic   exploitation   is
therefore   closely   connected   with   a   co-ordinated   and
harmonious development of all the elements of the regional
system [U.R.E., 1988].

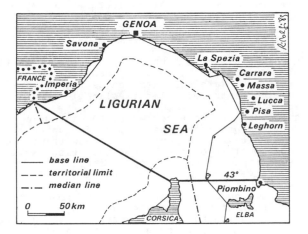

Figure 1. Limits of the Ligurian Sea.

       The coastal region of the Ligurian Sea can boast such
natural sceneries that most of the place names along it are
known world-wide: the Riviera of Flowers, the Western
Riviera, the Eastern Riviera and Versilia.
       The landscape rises on supporting lines generated by
the horizontal geometry of the large marine expanses in
clear contrast with the vertical geometry of the Alpine and
Apennine heights which plunge directly into the waters
(Liguria) or emerge at a short distance inland (Versilia)
where the white peaks of the Alpi Apuane back a narrow
coastal plain.
       Further south, the mouth of the river Arno with its
alluvial plain breaks out from nearby hills and then the
orography tapers down to hills fringing the slightly curved
coastline.
       There is a mingling of shapes, volumes and colours
scanned with the rhythms of the furrowed Ligurian valleys,
open to the waterfront or underlined by the deep green of
the almost uninterrupted littoral stretches of   Tuscan
pinewoods.
       Everywhere there are historical landmarks   witnessing
an illustrious history (the Republics of Genoa and Pisa) or
a humbler history of centuries of man's hard labour as in
the fishing village of Noli, Camogli, Portovenere, in the
terraced slopes of the Cinque Terre and drainage and
reclamation in the Tuscan coastal plains.

Watch-towers, against the dangers of piratical raids, and sanctuaries, for invoking divine protection, recall the anxieties and hopes of daily life in ancient times.

The mildness of the climate favours olive groves, the ancient symbol of the area, today complemented with a newer emblem: the exotic flora of parks and gardens.

In order to meet the demand for leisure, for many decades these natural assets have been complemented by a modern and efficient set of infra-structures for access by land (motorways, railways, airports) and by sea (commercial and touristic ports); of reception facilities and a complete range of services to meet all kinds of demands for leisure and entertainment.

And in this region the "supply model" almost meets the "demand model". In Liguria 1,500,000 inhabitants (85% of the region's population) are concentrated near the coast and here too are concentrated almost all of the region's productive activities.

From the mouth of the river Magra to Viareggio, a line of urban development backs the shore for about thirty kilometres. This area is supported by a network of tourist attractions as well as by other manufacturing activities (medium and small industries) and by agriculture which over the years has evolved into a highly rewarding business with the cropping of vegetables and flowers.

In the remaining stretch of the Tuscan coast the towns of Pisa, Leghorn and Piombino alternate to less densely urbanised areas including minor centres with a robust economic vitality, arising from recent industrial and commercial initiatives, based on the traditionally rich agriculture.

Taken as a whole, the coastal zone of the Ligurian Sea bears a demographic load of three million inhabitants distributed throughout the eight provinces of Imperia, Savona, Genoa, La Spezia, Massa-Carrara, Lucca, Pisa, Leghorn. Extending the calculation to the entire population of the two coastal regions (Liguria and Tuscany) and to at least half of those in the bordering inland regions (Piedmont, Lombardy, Emilia-Romagna) it can be estimated that the potential national demand amounts to not less than ten million inhabitants to which - to complete the picture - should be added a few other millions of persons representing the potential foreign demand mainly coming from Germany, Switzerland, Great Britain and France.

All of these regions and countries have in a high degree requirements which regulate the formation of an effective touristic supply.

The merging of these favourable factors has led to the "exploitation" and then the touristic "occupation" of the coastal region, starting from the last century, when the Ligurian Rivieras became for distinguished foreign travellers basic stops of their Italian tours.

In this area originated élitarian tourism in "villas" which gradually added to the landscapes of the most well-known resorts: Bordighera, San Remo, Alassio, Santa Margherita, Rapallo, Lerici, Viareggio.

The fame of these names stimulated further exploitation of many other similar places, until almost the entire Ligurian Rivieras and Versilia were developed. During the inter-war period some of those places acquired an even greater and more diversified clientele, attracted for the ummer and winter seasons and by the new fashion of sea bathing.

After the second world war mass tourism was brought into being by the various factors mentioned above (1).

The consequent growth of receptive structures underwent considerable changes, producing a progressive development. Up to the beginning of the 1960s the effect of this was limited. It mainly was concentrated in the building of hotels and pensions in urban or suburban areas of centres already established or of centres where the tourist appeal was beginning to emerge.

During the first half of the 1970s the process tended to decrease in Liguria but continued in Versilia and along the coasts of Pisa and Leghorn. However, along with this, grew the new phenomenon of "second home", with small villas, condominiums and residences. The effect on the environment is considerable and often dramatic given that the resources of the countryside and its surroundings are considered simply as "expendable capital" [Bazzoni, 1986].

The establishment of longitudinal and transverse motorways contributed, during these years of considerable economic growth in the country, to permanent or temporary migrations towards the coast. In addition, the lack of restrictions led to uncontrolled proliferation of buildings: at first, at acceptable intervals along roads approaching the centres and along the sea front, then in an intensive way, in the available spaces within previously built areas. When front row building reached saturation or the cost of a "sea view" became too expensive, building was extended along hillsides, to the detriment of agricultural activities.

Recently, in many districts, hotels met difficulties because of the excessive proliferation of secondary homes. In Liguria, for example, from 1970 to the present day, 700 hotels have been closed: for the most part because they were over 50 years old or because deluxe classes of the first decades of the century no longer were adequate to meet present day demands.

----

1) As an example it is worth recalling that in Italy free time available for every citizen has increased during this century from 11% to 39% while labour time has decreased from 56% to 28%. With the advantage of increased earnings the use of free time for tourism and leisure activities has increased considerably in the last thirty years. Holidays of Italians and other Europeans have been tripled in number of days, reaching in 1986 349 million days of holidays with 99 million days spent in hotels and other similar accomodation. The tourist industry employs 8% of the work force which increases to 13% when ancillary employment is included [Preger, 1986].

The Tuscan coast has also been involved in similar development processes. However, here the building came a little later and has been less harmful and more green areas are visible. The accessibility to the shore south of Leghorn is rather difficult as the autostrada has not been built up to here; access is through the Via Aurelia, which is narrow and often runs through built-up areas.

The general degradation of the environment results in a negative effect on tourism. While an unspoiled environment is attractive a degraded one arouses repulsion in the visitor, who inevitably turns to other less "consumed" areas to satisfy the demand for leisure and entertainment [Preger, 1986].

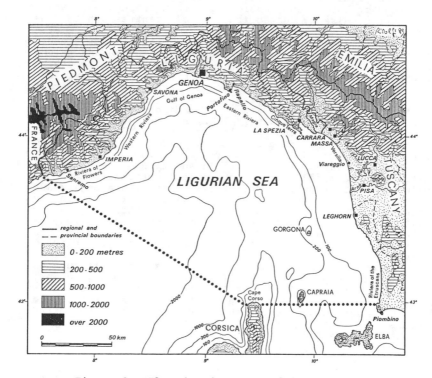

Figure 2.   The Ligurian Sea and its coast.

All these processes can be noted along the coast of the Ligurian Sea, although the intensity decreases from north to south.   The situation is more serious in the Ligurian Rivieras because the space available on the waterfront is partly devoted to railways and roads, dense urban building, numerous commercial ports·and marinas, hotels close to the beaches and bathing establishments [Leardi, 1982; Vallega, 1982].

The concentration of these uses continues in Versilia (that is from Forte dei Marmi to Viareggio) with the same intensity but with a lower density of buildings. Here, a 4-5

km wide stretch of flat land is available, which has
favoured the distribution of uses along wider stretches   and
parallel lines.

        In fact, proceding from inland we can   recognise a
series   of old centres (Massa,   Carrara,   Pietrasanta,
Seravezza,   Camaiore)   lined along the foot   of   the Apuan
mountains and located on conoids or hillsides for protection
from the hazards of the sea (piratical raids) and from   the
plain   (stagnant   marshy waters).   These are linked by   the
railway (Pisa-La Spezia) and by national road number 1   (Via
Aurelia).
        Then there is a low intermediate plain, lying   between
the elevated contours and the   coast, partly peaty and   once
subject to flooding (the lake of Massaciuccoli).   Due to
reclamation, this is intensely cultivated (cereals,   forage,
vegetables, flowers) and is gradually being built, although
the type of construction respects the need for   green   open
spaces.
        Finally, the stretch nearest the sea hosts,   amid
residual areas of pinewoods, the lining up of beach   resorts
which have been established as tourist-residential areas and
tend to duplicate along the shore the   inland   centres
which have made the region famous (Marina di Massa,   Marina
di Carrara, Marina di Pietrasanta, Lido di Camaiore).
        Further south, other resorts have been   established
recentely which are already important in the tourist economy
of the Tuscan coast.   Between Pisa and Leghorn,   the
pinewoods of Tirrenia host the seaside resort which is   in
continuous expansion. South of Leghorn, the centres   of
Quercianella   and Castiglioncello have   a   consolidated
tradition for offering the green of the Mediterranean
scrubland and of the pine woods to new   residential
quarters.
        The remaining stretch of coast between Cecina and   the
Promontory of Piombino, shows good prospects for future
development. In recent decades within the limits of   the
woods and   beaches, marinas and holiday villages have
been established, as Marina di Cecina, Bibbona a Mare,
Marinetta and Donoratico a Mare [Innocenti, 1987].
        The modern architecture of small villas, hotels   and
blocks of flats has not been too harmful to green areas   of
the littoral pinewoods, which for long stretches are   still
intact and subject to regulations, as is the case beyond San
Vincenzo, in the Gulf of Baratti and on the steep Promontory
of Populonia, where a dense natural wood of Mediterranean
scrub conceals the remains of the ancient inhabitants: the
Etruscans.

The use of the sea for tourism and leisure

        As we have seen tourism has been a very important
factor - although not the only one - in recent settlement
processes along the Ligurian coast. Tourism is responsible
for the intensification of the role of the sea in the
perception of the people.

    More than ever, the coastal sea may be regarded an
essential element of the cultural landscape. For efficient
management of these marine areas new cultural approaches are
required.   The same that are necessary for the protection of
the environment in general [Zunica, 1986].
    In order to understand the essential elements of the
human behaviour-marine environment relationship in   the
Ligurian Sea, it would be useful to examine first the
"functions" of this sea (i. e. the effects it casts on the
coastal region and its inhabitants) and then the "uses" of
it.
    Uses, in particular those connected with recreational
tourist activities, can be ascribed to a horizontal
coordinate which distinguishes between coastal   sea
(contained within the limits of the continental plateau) and
deep sea, and a vertical coordinate, which distinguishes
between marine surface, the mass of water, the sea bed, and
the subsoil (fig. 3).

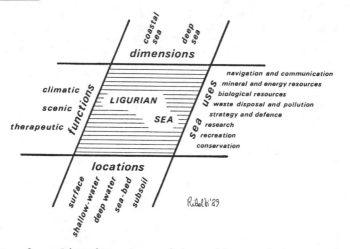

**Figure   3.   Ligurian Sea: interactions between human
         activities and marine environment.**

    On considering first the various functions, it is
noted that the "climatic" role is particularly accentuated
in the case of the Ligurian Sea not only because of its
latitude but also because of the notable quantity of water
in this sea (more than half of the area is from 1000 to
2500 m deep) and by the conformation of the basin, enclosed
to the north and east by a range of mountains. The long
coastal stretch therefore enjoys very favourable climatic
conditions in the summer as well as in the winter, when the
mountains enclosing it provide protection from cold north
winds (fig. 2) (2).

----
2) In Genoa the annual average maximum temperature is
18.5° C. The annual average minimum temperature is 12.5° C.
The annual average rainfall is 954 mm. The annual average
number of rainy days is 76.

Just as the climatic function depends on the mass of water so the "scenic" role is connected with the marine surfaces, extending from the shores to the distant horizon. The sea, with its changing of colours, with the movement of the waves, with its luminosity, is pleasantly perceived by humans. In all of its manifestations there is a recreational potential easily perceivable by everyone.

The scenic function, however, has different elements, according to whether the marine surface is bordered by a low and uniform coast or whether, in contrast, there is a rugged morphology with oblique or vertical dominant lines. In the latter case, the landscape acquires important scenic values with differing effects of shape, colour and depth in the field of vision.

The whole Ligurian shore and for that of Tuscany, south of Leghorn and near Piombino, enjoy to a great extent this particular scenic function. Besides a generally high degree of recreational interest, these coastal stretches offer in certain areas (Promontory of Portofino, the Cinque Terre) an explicit tourist attraction, as they are destinations for day trips by land or by sea.

The "therapeutic" function of the sea, nowadays referring especially to the atmosphere, since in certain periods and places bacteriological conditions of the water are beyond acceptable limits. This function has been in the past the main attraction for prolonged summer and winter stays in seaside resorts.

The discussed functions relate to the physical aspects of the sea and therefore constitute general characteristics of this element which are present in different combinations and with differing effects in all oceans.

Instead, the concept of "use" implies a direct or indirect action of man involving the sea; therefore uses have not always been the same in terms of time as they are not the same in space. They vary in number and intensity according to cultural, economic and technological level of human groups and therefore also according to the quality and quantity of the needs expressed by these groups. Needs that are notoriously expressed in a graded order, not only because of spontaneous requests but also as a result of economic and political stimulations [Fabbri, 1985].

This is particularly pertinent to tourist and recreational activities. The intense use of the sea to these aims is in fact a recent process related to improved standard of living. It comes alongside the historic uses such as fishing and navigation with which grounds for conflict may arise when present in the same waters.

Most of marine uses for leisure take in fact place along a very limited coastal strip, a few hundreds of metres wide and only tens of metres deep. This is the most delicate part of the sea. Being in contact with the land, it suffers directly from mans's activities. The more intense these are, the more the sea is likely to suffer from ecological problems.

Where man lacks respect for the land where he lives this is apt to deteriorate. We well know what this means for leisure activities connected with the sea since nowadays the slogan offering a "clean sea" and a "clean beach" for holidays is being used world wide.

The Ligurian Sea has these complex problems. Above all, in connection with recreational activities such as bathing, surfing, fishing, snorkel, deep dea diving, water skiing.

On considering activities within the function of the morphological characteristics of the coast, it is possible to identify two different types. Low sandy coasts are well available for mass sea- and sun-bathing especially where wide beaches and shallow waters are present. On the contrary, cliffy coasts offer much less accessibility and convenience for bathers, especially in the case of non swimmers.

The waters on these coasts are instead particularly suitable for other recreational activities such as fishing, deep sea diving and under-water swimming. These activities depend on the availability of benthos in limpid and clean waters.

The coastal belt south of the river Magra, is quite suited to the use of bathing. Here this use has been highly developed and for many years the shores have been saturated with buildings and services. Along the Tuscan littoral only two short stretches are still undeveloped: the sandy stretch between the outlets of the rivers Serchio and Arno, which was not accessible because it was part of the estate of S. Rossore, which has been until recently a property of the Italian Presidency; and the rocky stretch south of Leghorn.

The whole Ligurian coast can be classified as cliffy except for a few and very short stretches. For this area, consequently, rather than "suitability" one should speak of "adaptability" to the function of bathing resort. This, in fact, is normally congregated in gravelly bays, formed by streams and river outlets. The small flat areas lying behind the shore are usually occupied by villages located very close to the coastline and excluding any possibility of further development for bathing establishments.

Therefore in the case of the coast of Liguria the use of the sea for bathing is limited within narrow natural strips. In compensation, favourable conditions exist here for underwater activities which, on the contrary, find little attractions in the uniformity of sandy low-lying coasts.

Excellent conditions for underwater swimming and deep sea diving are offered by those stretches of coast that are so high that it is impossible or difficult to reach them by land and which rapidly descend into depths of 30-50 m and thus making it possible to observe Mediterranean fauna and flora.

In the Ligurian Sea places that respond to these requirements and have therefore acquired some fame in underwater sporting circles are the Promontory of Portofino, the zone of the Cinque Terre (from Manara Point to Mesco Point, to Portovenere, to the island of Palmaria), the zone from Vado Ligure to Bergeggi and to Capo Mele, the Gorgona and Capraia Islands, the promontories of Piombino and of Cape Corso.

These uses of the sea are also subject to the variability of season. It is obvious that the summer season in general favours all touristic-recreational activities connected with the sea. Undoubtedly it influences the bathing season, limiting it to the period of June to September. But underwater activities are free from seasonal influence given the special protective equipment in use.

For both uses the "state of the sea", as can easily be understood, is most important. For amateur or sporting fishing the season is instead regulated by biological cycles and migrations.

The state of the sea and weather conditions are even more important for nautical sports as sailing, windsurfing, waterskiing, yacht racing, yacht cruising. Since there are no precise limitations of space these sports are widely practised during summers and main holiday periods. This applies above all to vessels which are fit for long cruises. Smaller vessels, sailing boats or motor boats, authorized to sail within a six-mile limit, are at sea mainly in the summer, but they also appear in other seasons, on public holidays and at week-ends.

Besides the type of licence granted to the boat, the distribution of this use of the sea depends on two factors: the presence, along the coast of mooring facilities, as well as particular points of atraction (islands, gulfs, bays, caves) which can be preferred destinations.

Leisure time spent on sea is increasing in popularity everywhere in the area and many marinas and small ports (43 along the Ligurian coast and 15 along that of Tuscany) are already over their mooring capacity. As a result, there are more boats on the sea and during the summer navigational difficulties arise in those particularly popular areas where at the same time there are excursion boats running along fixed lanes fulfilling tourist demand during holiday seasons (Paradiso Gulf, Tigullio Gulf, La Spezia Gulf) or regular daily public services for places with no means of communication by land (Punta Chiappa, S. Fruttuoso).

The Ligurian Sea has within limits also facilities for cruises. The port of Genoa is of primary importance as landing point for Mediterranean tours (similarly to Naples and Venice) and normally it is used by some 300 cruise ships a year. In addition to the routes which cross the Ligurian Sea there are several places along its coast which are popular destinations for tourist ships.

The Gulf of Tigullio and particularly the waters outside Portofino are visited every year by tens of cruise ships (in 1988 there were 54), staying at anchor for 2 or 3 days with passengers enjoying visits to the shore. Viareggio and Leghorn also welcome every year cruise ships touring the Ligurian and Tyrrhenian Sea with cruises including the Cote d'Azur, Corsica, Island of Elba, Versilia, Ligurian Rivieras. When in port cruise ships organize day-visits to nearby cities of major tourist attraction, such as Lucca, Pisa, Florence.

Final remarks

As we have seen, the whole coastal stretch of the
Ligurian Sea displays considerable aesthetical and
environmental values which justify a good ground for
touristic-leisure activities. The forms of this use and
their distribution call for environmental conditions
sufficiently fit.

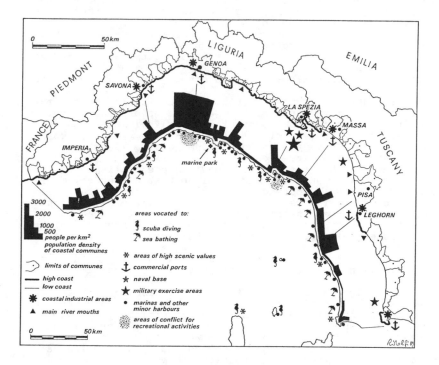

Figure 4. Model of sea uses in the Ligurian Sea.

Along the coast the environment must be protected from
being spoilt by often irresponsible human impact, as has
happened in many places. Equally, the marine environment
has to be protected and restored to a biological equilibrium
for a safe approach to all uses regarding leisure and the
exploitation of the biological resources.

These are some of the topics concerning the management
of the sea. For a better understanding, it would be useful
to conclude with an examination of functional compatibility
existing among different uses of leisure time on sea and
other uses. To this aim, we can classify existing
relationships as beneficial, indifferent and conflicting
[Doumenge, 1981; Walker, 1987].

The Ligurian Sea includes all eight categories of use classified in The Times Atlas of the Oceans (1983). In particular, 25 out of the 29 main uses listed in the classification are in operation, with the absence in this sea of separation lanes and installations for extraction of hydrocarbons and minerals.

Of the uses of leisure time, which amount to 8 in the cited Atlas, the important activity of under-water swimming has been developed in recent years in Italian waters, as well as nautical activities as sailing and motor boating.

In the Ligurian sea, and in particular along 500 kms of coastal waters, the 8 uses of leisure time co-exit with about twenty other uses in beneficial or indifferent conditions in some cases (with demersal or pelagic fishing, submarine archaeology, scientific research, submarine parks, preservation zones) and in conditions of conflict in others (military zones, river discharges, urban sewage, industrial outfalls).

The resulting model is very complex and hazardous, as models of other densely populated Italian and Mediterranean shores. The complexity derives from the great variety of uses and from high densities. The risk - for the marine environment in general and for leisure activities in particular - lies in the impossibility of reaching a complete differentiation in zones including only integrated uses.

When this does not occur the relations between incompatible uses give rise to conflicts which accentuate the risk [Vallega, 1987]. Symptoms of this condition can be seen in many coastal places along the Ligurian Sea. The most notable are always connected with the most extreme forms of human intervention along the coast.

The merging of actions produced by a heavy load of population on the coastal environment has led to deterioration gradually approaching a non-reversible status of the delicate equilibriums of the sea.

On the basis of these considerations, the general model of recreational uses in the Ligurian Sea can be divided into two sections virtually corresponding to the regions of Liguria and Tuscany.

In the first section, the Ligurian area, from the French frontier to the mouth of the River Magra with a high coastline and deep waters bearing a demographic load of 1,500,000 inhabitants (4,700 inhabitants per km of coastline concentrated in 63 littoral communes), half of which grouped in a large city (Genoa) and the remainder distributed throughout a hundred or so coastal towns recreational uses of the sea co-exist with all other uses.

Along the Rivieras the reasons for conflict are limited and generally confined to waste disposal. In the central section of the coast (Gulf of Genoa) however, the conflict reaches a maximum level because of the concentration, along the water front, of a wide range of uses connected with urban, industrial and port functions. Another critical point is the Gulf of La Spezia and the waters surronding it.

The motives of conflict present in the Gulf of Genoa

are somewhat reduced here but there are additional special uses for military exercises associated with La Spezia being the second largest naval base in Italy (naval dockyards, surface warships, submarine exercise areas, firing/bombing ranges) [Ridolfi, 1988].

The second section, that of Tuscany, with a low coastline and a gradually widening continental plain (up to 30-40 km inland from the shore) with a still high demographic load (3,700 inhabitants in 18 littoral communes), but inferior to that of Liguria, equally disposes of recreational uses of sea as well as a great deal of other uses.

As we have said, the littoral urban network is more sparse and as a result the motives for conflict, along the coast and in the sea, are reduced and are localised at the major river mouths (Arno, Serchio) and in the town of Leghorn, where urban, industrial and port functions merge together.

Along the remaining continental and insular coastlines (Gorgona, Capraia, the extremity of Capo Corso) recreational activities are often intensely developed in environmental conditions that are in general still good even though here too there are dangers of conflict, with incompatible uses of local origin or coming from nearby coastal areas.

In recent years, in Italy, however, the number of protective measures concerning the sea have been developed, especially in the Ligurian Sea. Many public and private bodies are firmly committed to these policies and the Governement itself promulgated, in 1984, a law for the defence of national waters.

Now, as never before, the life of the sea depends on the goodwill of man.

USE OF SEA FOR LEISURE   125

References

BAZZONI, R.: Coste e litorali. In: Annuario Europeo
dell'Ambiente 1986, pp. 201-211. Docter ed., Giuffrè,
Milano, 1987.

DOUMENGE, F.: Problemes de l'amenagement integrè du
littoral méditerranéen. In: Management of living
resources in the Mediterranean coastal area, 58,
pp. 329-350. FAO, Studies and reviews, 1981.

FABBRI, P.: Lo spazio-spiaggia: usi ed erosioni. In: La
gestione delle aree costiere, 25, pp. 120-135.
Edizioni delle autonomie, Roma, 1985.

INNOCENTI, P.: Il turismo in provincia di Livorno. Aspetti
economici e commerciali, 2 voll., C.C.I.A.A. di
Livorno, Pacini, Pisa, 1987.

LEARDI, E.: La funzione turistica e gli insediamenti in
Liguria. In: Bollettino della Società Geografica
Italiana, suppl. vol. XI, 35-48 (1982).

PREGER, E.: Tempo libero e turismo. In: Annuario Europeo
dell'Ambiente 1986, pp. 864-866. Docter ed., Giuffrè,
Milano, 1987.

RIDOLFI, G.: Il mare proibito. Aspetti geografici degli usi
militari del Mediterraneo. In: Rivista Geografica
Italiana, VC, 2, 121-150 (1988).

THE TIMES: Atlas of the Oceans, Couper a., Times Books,
London, 1983.

UFFICIO DELLE RICERCHE ECONOMICHE: Da una politica
tradizionale del turismo a una politica turistico-
ricreativa integrata. In: Contributi d'analisi e di
politica turistica, pp. 1-32. Rapporti semestrali,
Bellinzona, 1988-II.

VALLEGA, A.: La Liguria marittima: riflessioni sulla
regionalizzazione litoranea. In: Bollettino della
Società Geografica Italiana, suppl. vol. XI,
9-15 (1982)

VALLEGA, A.: La gestione del mare. Problema del metodo. In:
Atti LIX Riunione SIPS, pp. 117-130. Genova, 1987.

WALKER, H.J.: The shoreline: realities and perspectives. In:
Coastal Planning: realities and perspectives, pp. 60-
82. Comune e Università, Genova, 1987.

ZUNICA, M.: Per un approccio con l'interfaccia terra-mare.
In: L'umanizzazione del mare, pp. 119-134. C.N.R.,
Roma, 1986.

Uses of the Sea for Leisure Activities in Italy

Sandra Vantini* - Maria Laura Pappalardo**

Summary

In the last ten years pleasure boating has undergone such a development that it can no longer be considered an exclusively elitarian phenomenon. The social and economic situation permits and suggests particular uses of leisure time to increasingly larger sections of the public. The increase in boating has been met by a suitable upgrading of port facilities which are under a legislation presently lacking. The planning of the tourist port network should constitute a valid support to the economy and therefore be a territorial factor of equilibrium, above all in the South.

Introduction

Italy, with a coastal development of over 8,000 kms and a structure which in some ways resembles a pier extending in the Mediterranean, seems vocated for seafaring. If in the past this has been more of a legend than a real experience of its people, in the last decades it has involved more and more extensive social aspects.

Beginning in the Sixties the increase in average procapita income has in fact resulted in a rise in tourist demand and this in turn has strengthened the need for alternative ways of spending leisure time. In particular seaside recreation has been extended to pleasure boating which, favoured by climatic conditions as well as the geographical situation already mentioned, can better fulfil the quest for freedom, relaxation and contact with nature which bathing is increasingly unable to satisfy because of the overcrowding of beaches.

To evaluate the extent of the phenomenon it will suffice to consider some figures. The annual production of pleasure boats rose from 9616 vessels in 1960 to 56,686 in 1981 and the register of boats in the same period records an increase of 85.3%. As can be seen the increase appears remarkable although the reference to official sources - The

---

* pp. 1-6 ** pp.7-12 Researchers, University of Verona, Faculty of Magistero, Institute of Geography, 37129 Verona.

Ministry of Mercantile Marine and the Ucina-Consornautica[1] -
only gives an approximate figure. In fact not all boats are
under an obligation to register and for a more accurate idea
one can only make an estimate.

Italian fleet craft.

    The development of boating has gained in the last
thirty years a considerable momentum along with the changing
needs of the consumers and through improved methods of
construction.   For these reasons official surveys have
adapted over the years the criteria for registration.   They
have moved from a rigid criterium which in 1970 obliged
42,764 boats to comply to regulations which lowered the
tresholds of obligatory registration to 6 meters or to 3
gross tons or to 20 hp. motor power (raised to 25 hp. in
1986)[2].

Tab. 1 -   List of boat types registered with the National
           Maritime Departments from 1960 to 1985.

	Motor boats and speedboats	Sailboats	Rowing boats	Total
1960	6,647	3,895	24,082	34,624
1963	11,733	4,187	29,180	45,100
1966	15,359	4,338	35,594	55,287
1969	19,792	4,315	41,346	65,453
1970	21,694	5,342	42,764	69,800
1973	43,239	9,845	41,199	94,283
1976	41,157	9,296	18,906	69,359
1979	44,412	10,289	9,824	64,525
1981	46,624	10,752	6,777	64,156
1983	61,856	12,721	1,605	76,182
1985	65,108	12,626	1,421	79,155

    Analysing the list of registered boats, it can be noted
that it has undergone a very remarkable increase especially
in the first decade.
    The significant trend is towards motor boats, the
number of which has tripled in the same period, with an
average annual increase of 12%.   In the three successive
years (1970 - '73) the increase has been so rapid as to
bring the total registered to 94,359.
    The increase in registration of sail boats is more
modest: 37% in the decade 1960 - '70 and 84% in the three
years of the boating "boom".   Consequently the ratio between
motor vessels and sailboats becomes more unfavourable for
the latter, changing from 1.7% (1960) to 4.4% (1973).
    After 1973 a decrease is noted involving every type of

enrolled vessel, due to the economic crisis. The subsequent
recovery reflects the trends previously seen and motor
crafts registered in the years 1973-'83 have an increase of
43%, against a 29% for sailboats.

There is a clear preference for motor boats, which
would be even more accentuated if one were to take account
boats registered under flags of convenience. It will be
interesting to check if small, and non-polluting sail boats
turns out to be penalised rather than the motor boat of
equal size.

Tab. 2 - Italian craft in the years 1985 - 1987.

		1 9 8 5	1 9 8 7	Increase %
Motor crafts	≤m. 7.5	49,600	51,000	2.8
	>m. 7.5	14,900	16,080	7.9
	Total	64,500	67,080	4.0
Sail crafts	≤m. 7.5	54,650	55,000	0.6
	>m. 7.5	11,650	12,179	4.5
	Total	66,300	67,170	1.3
Outboards and small boats		224,580	236,090	5.1
Dinghies		145,000	154,330	6.4
Sail boards		130,000	150,100	15.4
Total		630,380	674,770	6.5

If the estimates of the composition of the Italian
craft are taken into consideration, the slight numerical
weight of enrolled boats emerges clearly in comparison with
those vessels not subject to registration.

Different criteria of classification inhibit a
comparison with the trend examined earlier, but the
comparison of the estimates of 1985 - '87 allows a
consideration of the importance which pleasure boating
represents in the national economic framework.

Since larger boats and sail boats of every size
(excluding sailboards) emerge from this estimate as almost
in balance, their increase is different in the two years
considered (4% for motor vessels against 1.13% sail boats).
Moreover it compares with an higher increase for vessels
longer than 7.5 meters both for sail and motor. This trend
is however weighted as far as towards the motor boats with
the increase in small craft, counted separately, but all
obviously less than this length.

In the general increase the largest increment is totally due to small boats for reasons of convenience and taxation.

The techniques of construction (use of fibreglass or aluminium) have considerable reduced the costs, bringing it within reach of a vast number of people. Moreover, these boats usually are not obliged to be registered among taxable properties.

Small boats are mostly outboards and dinghies. Together with sailboards - whose recent spread has been very rapid - these constitute "equipment" connected with beach activities, allowing for short excursions off the polluted and crowded shore without further needs for special equipment for launching and towing.

Port facilities.

Boat users have at their disposal along Italian coasts 416 landing places (Pagine Azzurre, 1988), the features of which are very various. They can be sited on the shore or within navigable canals, and can be either public or private and variously fitted with services and infrastructures.

If from the total count achorages with rocks, jetties, single mooring posts are subtracted, and also all those for exclusive use of boating clubs, remain 241 ports with equipped berths (Fig. 1). These again show a vast range of situations. The ports can be run by Regional management, local authority or privately; they might be private developers or simply agents of the state structure.

Landing places are scattered in an irregular pattern and the average distance between them is of approximately 20 kms, or 33 Kms between those more specialised.

A numerical imbalance is noted between the first and second group and between the central-northern coasts and those in the south belonging both to the Adriatic-Ionian side and the Tyrrhenian.

There are a variety of reasons that explain this situation from those of the geomorphological character of the coasts to those related to poor accessibility which inhibits an increase in tourism in the hinterlands of southern ports.

Getting to regional cases landing places in Liguria (which is in the forefront of boating tourism thanks to its favourable geographical position) although overcrowded, are equipped with modern structures of a good standard.

In Tuscany where only two marinas have been established, there are numerous, but insufficiently equipped small ports, mainly because of the presence of islands and the need for connections between them and the mainland.[3]

In Latium the stretches of water suitable for boating

turn out to be inadequate for the demands of the huge and
profitable tourist business generated by the capital;
however a few marinas are under construction.

The landing places of Campania and of the islands in
the Gulf of Naples (only one marina) are overcrowded and not
intended specifically for boating.

Fig. 1 -   Distribution of tourist ports and harbours along
            the Italian coast.

The situation in Calabria and Basilicata is disastrous: in the whole developed coast there are only commercial ports, not always usable, and a few more minor landing places. On the Ionian coast only recently a marina has been set up, which is well-equipped and with good facilities.

Puglia has a wide range of ports insufficiently equipped, either in number or quality, for the needs of boating tourism.

Abruzzo and the Marche, excluding one marina, are without places specifically intended for pleasure boats, the small ports being at present only used for fishery activities.

Emilia-Romagna, even though setting up specialised landing places, has insufficient structures for its high tourist demand.

For Veneto and Friuli the situation seems near to ideal since the numerous installations are yet always efficient and, thanks to the availability of waterways and coastal lagoons, boating sites are suited to the needs of domestic and foreign tourism.

Considering the larger islands, Sardinia has specialised installations expanding rapidly, especially along the Emerald Coast. There are also numerous anchorages and shelters along high cliffy coasts, although not yet equipped for pleasure boats.

Along the long Sicilian coast, there are numerous ports but none of them is planned specially for pleasure boats.

The small pleasure boat, although mainly used at sea, has at its disposal in Italy numerous lakes. Analyses of the structures of the boating pleasure cannot ignore the situation of the inland waters, the facilities of which constitute an addition to those of the coast. In fact, very often the boating resident hinterland, chooses a fixed place on the lake for his own boat, usually using it at week-end and keeping it to take ot the sea for longer holiday periods. Later in winter, due to the fresh water, the need for storage becomes less pressing.

Complete information about boating places on the lakes doesn't exist, besides which there is considerable privatisation on the shores and access to the banks is often difficult because of morphological characteristics. The small ports in existence however are almost exclusively used for pleasure boating carried on almost everywhere on the lakes where fishing has declined and has no further commercial importance.

Port structures and legislation relating to harbour facilities.

From the brief look at the regional situation, one can

state that the necessary equipment for the development of boating is rather lacking in relation to the increased number of boats.

Specialised facilities are indispensable not only for yachts equipped to be autonomous. It should be realised nowadays, looking at the Italian boating scene, that an intermediate group of vessels has developed which is suited to coastal navigation. Shipyards can build cabin cruisers with good facilities, yet keep them within the sizes required for registration (Gomisceh 1987). Such vessels, require a structure and also a technical and logistical back-up service similar to those of the larger yachts and also slipways and shelters which are closer together, given their shorter autonomy and ability to deal with stormy sea conditions.

Presupponing that pleasure boating is a specialised activity, being no alternatives, for essential works people often turn to the equipment intended for merchant shipping. In Italy there still has not been an adjustment of port services to the needs of pleasure boats or leisure, which other competing Mediterranean countries - for example France - have set up, according to sophisticated criteria and yet with governmental incentives.

New ports which have been completed, although insufficient, are bound to clash with legislation dating back to 1885. Recent circulars from the Ministry of Marina Mercantile have sought to update the structures of boating tourism, still coming under the classification of Class IV ports, which is to say all those that are neither military nor commercial situated at the head of major communication[4] routes. Moreover, as the Navigation Code of 1942 reaffirms "the ports and the docks are part of State maritime property. The constructions which exist within the limits of state property and of territorial waters come under the jurisdiction of the State itself."

Only in July 1970, a "circular" takes into consideration the possibility of building and managing large port installations on the French model, intended for pleasure boats and with concessionary clauses which provides for sufficiently long time to recoup the expenses of construction.[5]

In the meantime, with the institution of the new Regioni, a presidential act (15th February 1972) also entrusts to the Regioni the "administrative functions relating to public works of regional benefit, including "the works concerning ports of the second category from Class II onwards." In 1977 another presidential act transferred to the regions the administrative functions for the maritime coasts, in the areas immediately overlooking state property on the lakes and rivers, when the foreseen use would have tourist and recreational ends". However the authority to decide on concessions remains still the central government. Therefore consistent progresses lack in the production of these tourist ports which in the early seventies one began to think of as a new possibilty for the development of the coasts.

The partial failure of these initiatives suggests in the end the growth of forms of smaller capacity which might be able to increase the possibility of receiving modest sized vessels, allowing in a relatively reduced time, the redemption of costs.

Such legislative deficiencies beside inhibiting the development of tourist ports, make also difficult any codification of them. The terminology itself doesn't make for clarity, often using indiscriminate expressions, such as "tourist port", "marina" and "landing place".

The most commonly used term is "tourist port" because even in its specificity, it is most generic. However it doesn't appear in the legislation which only distinguishes the military ports (first category) from the commercial ports (second category subdivided into I, II, III, IV classes)[6].

The term "marina" has various implications which implies services directed exclusively to tourist boating and to the boats through structures on land and at sea also including restaurants, recreational clubs, holiday villages.

The "landing place", on the contrary, implies the possibility of allocated berths and supplies. Yet, according to the circulars it can also be equipped with services and facilities for repair, maintenance, boat storage, servicing of vessels and also for short term stays and catering facilities for the boater.[7]

The "mooring points" instead are placed on mobile structures along the coast which allow the docking of boats and offer essential services such as jetties, cranes, deliveries, refuelling installations, water supplies, restaurants.[8]

From what has been stated it turns evident that an optimal classification of port facilities through the services offered might be inhibited by a legislation which, under different names, allong the existance of the same structures.

In Italy, to complicate things, the term marina recurrs frequently for places along the coast, often "budding" at major inland centres. Marina di Pisa is a good example whose canal port of the same name offers hospitality to various small docks for pleasure boats.

It must be underlined that the legislation allows that the completed places for boating can be managed by public bodies or by private management.

In general public landing places are included in commercial ports and are always described as "multi-functional". They have often constituted the first response to the increasing demand for mooring berths as such structures can use the services available for commercial ships. (Fig. 2)

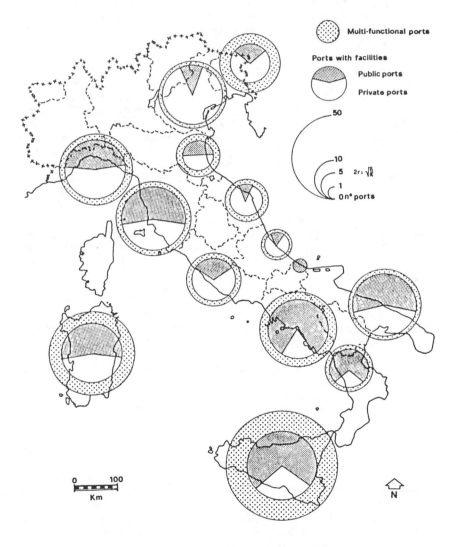

Fig. 2 - Port structures in single regions for comprehensive
         consistency, equipped for tourist boating and types
         of management.

Few of these public structures, built in the fifties, have been created for pleasure boating, yet, although not equipped with the more qualified services, they can use state grants to commercial ports of the IV class. At the beginning there were few towns with longstanding tourist interests which learned to recognise public the tourist interest.

In more recent times, through the institution of concessions, private organizations have assumed the initiative and the task of building landing places specifically intended for pleasure boats. The various sizes of these private structures derive from the financial capacity of the organizations, from the environmental situation, from the pool of customers (more or less large) and from regional plans for pleasure boating; which all these factors should take into account of in the overall planning of the territory.

Private participation has been prevailing, in comparison with public in the northern regions, where larger corporations of entrepreneurs has found co-operation and permissions.

In the south, on the contrary, places pleasure boating are mostly associated with public participation.

Environmental issues.

Ports and environment are often two irreconcilable things. There is no doubt that, if every structure, even one so modest as a small pier, has an impact on the land, still more will a tourist port bring about changes in the surrounding environment.

The impact of the use of the structure must be distinguished from that of its construction. If, in fact the former is controllable by man and therefore susceptible to modification in the course of time, the latter is permanent.

The concentration of boats in a limited area, presents certain positive aspects since it eliminates the problem of indiscriminate and illegal use of the coasts and allows control of pollution.

However the structure, the planning should be foreseen in its optimum extent. Whilst the tourist landing place can avoid the connections, positive and negative, with the activities taking place in the surrounding areas (since it contains such limited equipment as not to generate much effect, if any at all), the marina, for the services connected with it, must necessarily take account of the relations and of the impulses which it estabilishes with the economic and tourist structure its hinterland.

Tourist ports are often the initial pretext for

developing residential complexes and services where the
boating centre becomes one of many components in the tourist
business. There is the risk that these structures, often
totally aliens to the social life of the invested area, [9] do
not produce the expected economic benefits, causing only
negative results.

For this reason and also because of their excessive
size many projects have encountered opposition from various
social groups. [10] An example is the new port for 3.000 berths
which is under construction between S. Marinella and
Civitavecchia near to the terminal of the Roma-Civitavecchia
motorway: this project has not taken account of the
environmental conditions of the area, and has not been
preceded by any assessement of the environmental impact.
(Italia Nostra, Bollettino 258, May-June 1988)

If works of restructuring and enlargements are carried
out on already existing systems which have at their disposal
an urban hinterland, structures can be considerably
contained using those already exists. In this way the impact
on the area is minimal and one can achieve a revitalisation
of disused commercial ports which, to keep their original
function would need more solid assistance.

In the economically weak areas of the South, tourist
ports can also represent an opportunity for development and
encourage the construction of new infrastructures. The
surrounding territory could be positively involved by the
new developments, which though not necessarily large, should
be properly equipped with services.

The marina offers with its complex of services,
different types of jobs; the landing places need services
from the surrounding area, using those already existing or
new ones. These economic activities get to be available not
only for tourists but also for residents and can be used all
year round.

The planning and restructuring however must be directed
towards and overall co-ordination of the places for boating
so that their positioning and capacities can be intended as
points of strength in the local and national economy.

These are the bearings which have guided the special
plan for tourist ports in the Mezzogiorno, directed to the
completion of a network of slipways varying in quality and
purpose along the coasts so as to promote tourism in the
South.

On the contrary in the heavily developed tourist zones
where a good road system is already in existence, the
implementation of boating facilities aimed to economic
advantages, needs structures which must necessarily be
controlled. Otherwise there is the danger of overlanding the
system of infrastructures already present, creating further
overcrowding and deterioration.

Problems and perspectives.

In our society, in which an increasing percentage of income can be devoted to secondary needs, pleasure boating is destined to increase its importance. This trend is confirmed by the observations that the purchase of boats can be motivated by contrasting choices. If on the one hand the boat can be seen as a status symbol, on the other hand there are always many who see it as a means of satisfying personal needs, both physical and cultural, and a means to rediscover the environment.

It is clear that the problem of tourist ports will become more urgent and cannot be ignored: not only because of the economic importance which pleasure boatin has for boat-builders and for tourism, but also for the fragility of the Italian coastal system, which badly needs a global planning action.

To adapt the port system to tourist needs a revision of the legislation is vital, specifically as applied to tourist ports and including the institution of concessions, valid to maintain the State's rights over maritime property.

Private concession should not only favour individual interests but also a new way of managing an operation which affects the community. Yet there must also be a revision of the regulations regarding state management of ports which should not put too heavy encumbrances upon boating tourism in the commercial areas. (Acquarone, 1971)

Given the importance that tourism has for the whole Italian economy, both domestic tourist trends and international will have to be regulated carefully, avoiding in particular the risk that the flow of boating tourism might be directed towards the French and Yugoslav coasts or the Spanish and Greek coasts; that is towards ports which offer better services or which are less costly than the Italian ones.

If the northern coasts need above all a reorganisation encouraging pleasure boating to become an alternative to the use of the beach, in the South it needs be provided with the infrastructures necessary.

A co-ordination of the slipways would encourage the creation along Italian coasts of an effective pleasure-boat circuit, with benefits both for those of the Tyrrhenian basin as well as those of the Adriatic-Ionian basin.

For the new port units account will have to be taken also in a purely economic point of view, of the geographic problems of their positioning, no longer being able as in the past to ignore the deterioration of vegetation and excessive building. In fact the new awareness which is now widespread, makes it so that between the subjective motivations of tourist choice, the environmental consideration carries more weight.

The interests of environmental protection however, are not in contrast with those of pleasure boating, which would get heavy disadvantages from pollution. (Bonora, 1986)

In conclusion one must reaffirms the need for few regulations in respect of tourist boating, which in a clear and unambiguous form estabilish the procedures to be followed in order to achieve the fulfilment of the plan, and also making clear the various roles which decision-makers, whether by private or public rights, must have. Only so, through the pleasure boat and the facilities intended for it will one be able to improve the tourism in certain areas and to raice it in others: but if the natural space represents an essential component of leisure, even boating, in order to have a future, must not contribute to the deterioration of the environment and must be in tune with conservation.

Notes

[1] - Since 1960 the Ministry of Marina Mercantile has processed in a constant and regular way the data concerning the annual registration in the national maritime departments. The UCINA Consornautica estimates the yearly production of pleasure boats and, since 1970, also the overall composition of the Italian nautical scene.

[2] - Act No. 51, 6/3/1976 and Act No. 193, 26/4/1986.

[3] - The presence of several small archipelagos makes more numerous but not necessarily more specialised, the port developments of regions such as Tuscany, already mentioned, and Latium, Campania, Sicily and Sardinia.

[4] - Act 30/3/1942 No. 327, articles 28-29.

[5] - Circular of the Ministry of Marina Mercantile. General Management of State Maritime Property and Ports: "Construction of turist landing places for management with economic criteria", Rome 1970.

[6] - Royal Decree 2/4/1885 No. 3095. Act 16/7/1884, No. 2518, which covers ports, beaches, lighthouses from the earlier law 20/3/1865 on public works.

[7] - Circular of the Ministry of Marina Mercantile No. 154, 24/5/1975, Rome.

[8] - Circular of the Ministry of Marina Mercantile No. 172, 2/3/1978, Rome.

9
  - The Island of Albarella, organised as an exclusive
private club, constitutes a significant example of an
elitarian development, highly equipped, but disconnected
with the social reality of the Po delta, where it is
situated. Its tourist port, with 500 berths, is one of 5 in
Italy (102 in all Europe) which has received the recognition
of the Blue Flag given by FEE, (European Federation of
Environmental Awareness) on the basis of: purity of water,
absence of untreated sewage, cleanliness of the site,
provision of techincal security equipment, availability of
environmental information to the public, removal of boat
refuse. Yet this is not one of the places open to tourists.

10
  - Even from the point of view of whoever must redeem the
capital investment in the period allowed by the concession,
(50 years) the boating development becomes economical with
300 berths. Recent studies have indicated also the maximum
threshold for the Italian situation at around 1000 berths.

References

Acquarone, L.: La concessione di impianti turistici
    portuali. In A.A.C.S.T., Atti del Convegno Nazionale
    "Per un sistema dei porti turistici inserito nella
    realtà territoriale regionale e nazionale", Napoli
    (1971)

Bonora, P.: Degrado ambientale e nautica da diporto. In
    C.N.R., L'umanizzazione del mare, Roma (1986)

Gomiscech, B.: Il turismo nautico nel Friuli-Venezia-Giulia.
    In: Quaderni dell'Istituto di Geografia della Facoltà di
    Economia e Comemrcio, n. 7, Università di Trieste (1987)

Italia Nostra: Bollettino 258, maggio-giugno 1988. Italia
    Nostra, Roma (1988)

Pagine Azzurre: Guida internazionale al diporto nautico.
    Roma (1988)

The Italian Seas: Legal Frameworks and Management
Patterns

Adalberto Vallega *

Abstract

Italy played a leading role in promoting
agreements on the jurisdictional belts--continental
shelves--in the Mediterranean Sea. This was due to the
need for developing exploration and exploitation of oil
and gas resources and it was also a starting point for
the diffusion of sea uses and related environmental
impacts in marine areas with a high level of man-sea
interactions. This process has been developing since
the late Sixties and concerns jurisdictional belts
influenced by various features both from the tectonic
and geomorphological standpoints. The analysis tends to
face the relationships between: i. the setting up of
jurisdictional belts; ii. the increase of kinds of sea
uses; iii. the diffusion of environmental impacts. In
this context two management patterns of the sea are
drafted: the Tyrrhenian and the Adriatic models.

Discontinuous change

Among semi-enclosed seas, the Mediterranean has
threefold peculiarity: physical, due to the complex web
of tectonic plates and microplates; juridical, arising
from the numerous jurisdictional zone claims: economic,
as a result of the high density of land activities
involving marine areas and related environmental
impacts.

The consideration of the economic characters
should be the starting point of the analysis relating
to the phase of discontinuous change, which started in

* Adalberto Vallega, Istituto di Scienze Geografiche,
Università di Genova, Lungoparco Gropallo, 16122
Genova, Italia.

the   mid-Seventies,   involving   a   number   of   sea
activities,   as well as land activities producing sea
implications.

Among the main factors of change,   it should be
recalled that littoral industrialization, mainly based
on raw material transformation,   came to a stop;   the
importation of minerals and energy sources recreased
sharply in the seaport areas; littoral urbanization
in the most developed areas proceeded in a more gradual
way, indicating that the exponential growth-based model
ought   to   be   revised.   On the contrary,   the whole
Mediterranean has continued to attract tourists, and in
some areas like the islands,   Maghreb and Greece,   this
sector has shown a marked increase.

In   the   mid-Seventies   the   Suez   Canal   was
re-opened   and   the   Mediterranean   regained   its   past
accessibility.   Containerized traffic was particularly
advantaged   by   this   and,   especially   in   the   Southern
Range,   it spread very rapidly.   A set of strategies,
based upon transhipment functions of seaports, has been
applied   to   link   deep-sea   routes   with   feeder   routes.
Ports ranging between Algeciras-La Linea and Leghorn,
on the west,   and Trieste,   on the east,   have been the
most involved areas.

Up to 1975 offshore natural gas production was
limited   to   the   Ravenna   area   (Northern   Adriatic).
Drilling was taking place in various parts of the basin
but large production fields were only spotted in the
Gulf of Gabes (Tunisia).   Ten years later,   the Central
and Northern Adriatic seem to be fully exploited both
on   the   Italian   and   the   Yugoslavian side;   off   the
south-eastern coast of Sicily, wells over 200 m deep on
the sea-bed are being installed for oil production; the
exploitation   of   the   Gulf   of   Gabes   fields   is   in
progress;   off Castellon (Spain) operations are being
enacted to exploit a vast oil-field;   in several other
areas,   exploration and drilling leases have been
granted.

As far as biological resources are concerned on
the   basis   of   conventional   activities--breeding   of
oysters and other molluscs along French coasts,   eels
and mullets in the Po delta--a diffuse tendency to
extend them was initiated in the late Seventies with
total or partial fish-breeding and the establishment of
experimental   centres.   At   present   initiatives   and

projects tend to multiply and spread. In particular, Italy is planning methods of breeding based on the use of water discharges from power plants.

Naval uses of the basin have been moving from a phase dominated by East-West confrontation to a more complicated phase in which other factors are involved: (1) military pressure partly related to the strategies of terrorism, which are shown by bilateral conflicts (e.g. USA-Libya); (2) conflicts over territorial marine limits (e.g., Greece-Turkey) and exclusive fishery zones; (3) tensions within the Arab world; (4) risks occurring to air transport also over the sea. These situations create a rather delicate balance between naval use and other uses of the Mediterranean. Conflicts, naval drilling operations and pollution by vessels are the most evident consequences.

Lastly, waste disposal has become the most crucial and dangerous among sea uses. The main European rivers discharging into the Mediterranean--Ebro, Rhone, Po--flow through urban and industrial areas and thus considerably contribute to marine pollution. On the other side, because of the Aswan Dam, the Nile has notably reduced its supply of nutritive substances negatively affecting phytoplancton resources of Eastern Mediterranean. Two areas are more subject to pollution: the band between the Gulf of Valencia and Leghorn--which involves the southern part of the Balearic Basin, the Tyrrhenian Basin and the Ligurian Sea--and the Adriatic. Eutrophication and pollution based on mercury, arsenic and organic substances are diffusing.

Sea uses framework

In this context, new sea uses are developing and conventional ones are spreading in the Italian marine jurisdictional belts. As a consequence, conflicting and hazardous relationships between uses are strengthening and diffusing with increasing implications for environment and ecosystems.

In general, it could be stated that in the mid-Seventies the Mediterranean Sea entered into a phase of discontinuous change, in which its management has to deal with an increasing number of alternatives. This change and its related bifurcations in processes involving sea management and ecosystems differ according to the areas and specific land-sea relationships. Along Italian coastal belts change is

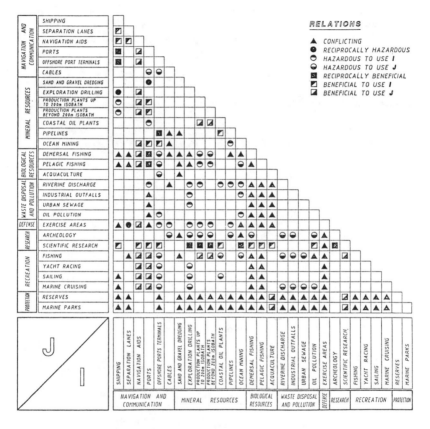

Figure 1. The web of uses in the Mediterranean Sea

developing to the point of producing the risk of
collapse in some marine areas, such as the Northern and
Central Adriatic. In fact, at present the following
eight categories of sea uses are being pursued in the
Mediterranean as a whole: 1. navigation and
communication; 2. mineral resources; 3. biological
resources; 4. waste disposal and pollution; 5. defence;
6. research; 7. recreation; 8. protection.

All of these do apply to Italian seas and the
hazardous relationships between uses and environment
are diffused. As a first approach the present situation
could be summarized in figure no. 1.

Relationships between uses have been identified
on the basis of qualitative criteria, taking into
account the data deduced from the literature. The
Mediterranean framework of uses not only induces us to
consider this matrix as a first approach, but it could
even cast a shadow of confutability over the results
obtained. Given these limits, the matrix can lead to
the following general deductions.

1. Planning and management. Compared with other
    semi-enclosed seas, such as the North Sea or the
    Caribbean Sea, Italian seas--and the Mediterranean
    Sea as a whole--fall behind in two ways. Firstly, in
    the field of management where initiatives are
    sectorial and quite different from area to area so
    that a lot has to be done before it will be possible
    to accomplish a global government of uses and the
    environment. Secondly, inasmuch as there are few
    initiatives in this direction, such planning has an
    experimental nature and concerns very limited areas.

2. Frequency of relations. Relations between uses are
    numerous because of the wide range of factors in
    terms of high densities of population, seaports,
    industrial structures and recreational activities.

3. Conflicting and hazardous relations. In comparison
    with other semi-enclosed seas the framework between
    uses in the Italian seas seems more articulated in
    terms of hazardous relations. For this reason, the
    area should be classified as a highly critical one.

4. Coastal zone. Literature has shown how, today, the
    coastal zone is defined in different ways according
    to countries and coastal regions. In each case
    certain factors are being emphasized: physical
    characters, environmental units, administrative

boundaries, arbitrary distances of the coastline or
of the baseline. This has not been faced for Italian
seas--and for the Mediterranean Sea as a
whole--either in a systematic way by the literature,
or by decision-making centres. Relations between the
shore and the sea in the context of the coastal zone
have been examined: 1. for particular uses such as
beach   defence   structures,   waste   disposal,
aquaculture, etc.; 2. when problems have emerged in
the   environment   and   in   the   framework   of
juridisdictional belts.

Jurisdictional zones

As   to   legal   factors   arising   from   the
international Law of the Sea, the Mediterranean
framework is changing. In the Seventies, the coastal
states redefined their baselines. When Suez re-opened,
Italy agreed on the median line of a large part of the
Adriatic continental shelf with Yugoslavia. This treaty
(1968) is the first of a sequence of agreements by
which, by the mid-Eighties, the Mediterranean Sea was
practically shared out. This sequence includes the
following treaties:
1. Italy-Yugoslavia, 1968: continental shelf;
2. Italy-Tunisia, 1971: continental shelf;
3. Italy-Spain, 1974: continental shelf;
4. Italy-Greece, 1977: continental shelf;
5. Libya-Tunisia: 1977, submission of the question of
   the continental shelf to the International Court of
   Justice; 1982, judgement of the International Court
   of Justice;
6. Libya-Malta, 1985: continental shelf.

Obviously the territorial sea is redefined
almost everywhere: all states have claimed their
exclusive fishery zone and some even delineated the
contiguous zone.

The claim to exclusive economic zones is
regarded as a delicate political problem and Western
European countries seem to believe that--at least at
the present time--such delimitations should not be
applied. However the risk of some non-European
Mediterranean countries doing so is serious. On the
other hand, this baseline definition is in itself a
cause of international tensions which are acute in the
Gulf of Sirte and less so for the Gulf of Taranto.

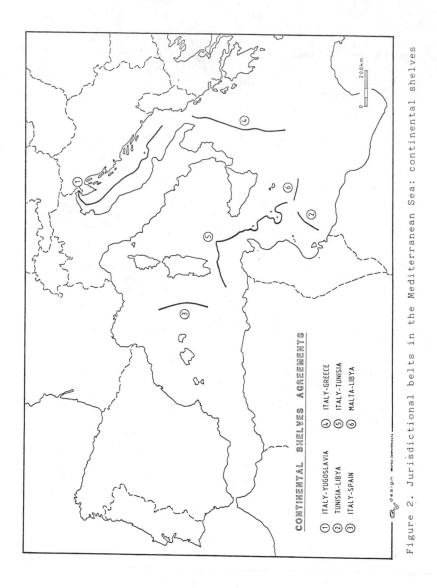

Figure 2. Jurisdictional belts in the Mediterranean Sea: continental shelves

Management patterns

As to some deductions that can be sketched about the management of the Italian seas, it seems appropriate to recall a few facts.

As far as physical features are concerned, the best solution would be offered by two management patterns. The first would concern the coastal zone and would be applied up to the outer edge of the continental margin. The second one would concern the deep-sea and ought to be developed through co-operation between Italy and other littoral Mediterranean countries. It is useful to recall that the continental margin is only wide in the Adriatic Sea, with more than 2/3 of its seabed extention, consisting of the shelf--and that the rest of the Mediterranean consists of large slopes and rises or abyssal areas.

As far as jurisdictional zones are concerned, Italy has power to develop uses and protection in every section of its marine environment--surface, water column, seabed and subsoil--only within its territorial limits, i.e. up to 12 nautical miles from baselines. Beyond this limit, the uses involving the seabed and subsoil could only be developed within the continental shelf--i.e. in the marine areas agreed as mentioned above. Up till now, Italy has promoted agreements relating to marine areas productive for the oil and gas industry. But it should be stressed that--as the involvement of the sea in economic activities increases--the need to claim its right over other marine spaces should come to the fore.

On the basis of these factors--physical and legal--two management patterns could be envisaged: 1. the agreed continental shelf is not extended to the limit of the continental margin; 2. the agreed continental shelf involves only the continental margin.

The first occurs in some western Mediterranean areas, i.e. in the Tyrrhenian Sea; the second expecially refers to the Adriatic.

These patterns could be conventionally referred to as "Tyrrhenian model" and "Adriatic model". They are to be regarded only as first approach models, to be implemented and arranged when specific areas are taken into consideration.

The Adriatic model involves marine areas with large continental margins so the agreed continental shelf only concerns the continental margin. It occurs in: 1. the Adriatic Sea to the north of the Gargano Peninsula; 2. the Ligurian Sea from Genoa westward; 3. the southern section of the Tyrrhenian Basin. Considering the agreed continental shelves between Italy and the Balcanic countries, it is possible to draft plans and develop management concerning: 1. the entire marine environment up to 12 nautical miles from the baselines; 2. only the seabed and subsoil from this limit up to the agreed boundaries of the continental shelf. Coastal zones only should be managed.

The Tyrrhenian model involves marine areas with narrow continental margins so the agreed continental shelf concerns both the continental margin and the deep seabed. It occurs in most of the Italian seas. Three management patterns can be envisaged: 1. up to 12 nautical miles from the baselines the entire set of uses can be implemented; 2. from this limit, up to the outer edge of the continental margin, Italy can develop uses concerning only the seabed and the subsoil; 3.from the outer edge of the continental margin up to the agreed boundaries of the continental shelf, Italy can develop uses concerning the seabed and the subsoil, but at the present time appropriate technologies are not available; as a consequence, only the protection and preservation of the marine environment can be pursued.

Pattern 1) involves the coastal zone management; patterns 2) and 3) involve the deep-sea management--of course in a complex and problematic way.

Final remarks

This approach to Italian seas--and the Mediterranean Sea as a whole--leads to emphasize certain points to which literature is paying a growing attention.

1. Theoretical research--properly based on research developed in several marine areas--is required to pursue better taxonomical criteria to classify sea uses. Bearing in mind that single uses converge to produce kinds of uses, and these converge to bring about categories of uses, it would be fit to offer theoretical frameworks on taxonomical criteria.

2.   The relationship between uses implies both
theoretical   and   methodological   questions.
Theoretical ones concern the definition of relations
and criteria by which the categories of relations
should be defined. The methodological ones concern
the criteria by which the measurement of the
relationships could be implemented.

3.   Environmental impact assesments require that
attention should be paid to the need to investigate
the feed-back relations involving only physical
features or both physical features and social
behaviour--bearing in mind that at the present time
retroaction is the category of relations which needs
to be evaluated from both the theoretical and
methodological standpoints.

4.   Diachronic analysis concerning the development of
the network of sea uses and the environmental
impacts becomes more and more relevant to the
building   up   of   scenarios   and   managerial
methodologies.

5.   In order to provide management patterns it would be
appropriate to look for a close connection between
regional science--regarded as a field of research
well endowed with conceptual and methodological
frameworks--and ocean sciences.

6.   Lastly, it seems clear that precious help could be
offered by the theory of complexity and related
concepts and methodologies. Nevertheless it should
be admitted that only a few steps have been explored
by the literature in this direction.

Historical Evolution of the Coastal Settlement in Italy: Ancient Times

Stefano Torresani[*]

Abstract

This contribution is aimed to follow the coastal demographic trend in peninsular Italy in the ancient and medieval age.

About 65% of these 3,500 km of shores are formed by a low cost, subject in the period to deep changes wich had important consequences on human settlement. Up to the beginning of the XX century these coasts have shown a trend to progradation due to siltation by rivers, thus resulting often swampy. This is why original settlements privileged high coasts, turning to the low ones only when watercourse controls and farming techniques for lowlands were acquired. The density of settlement may be evaluated only with homogeneous and sufficiently reliable statistical data: in Italy such conditions only date back to the 1800s. For earlier times the analysis must necessarily rely on qualitative trend evaluations, although demographic dimensions of some coastal cities are occasionally witnessed by historical or archaeological sources.

Most fossil findings relevant to the earliest man presence in Italy come from rocky coastal areas (fig. 1): it can therefore be supposed that these areas were privileged for milder climatic conditions and wider range of food resources (shellfish). The findings - dating back to the middle Palaeolithic - are concentrated in the vicinities of caves or lagoons. Man's presence along coast was occasional starting from about 300,000 years B.P., while the first settlement is documented 40,000 years B.P. (fig. 2). Favourable conditions for cave settlement are evidenced by the continuity in the findings up to the Neolithic period along (Radmilli, 1978). Coastal areas were also privileged pathway along which, starting from 8,000 years B.P., the Neolithic revolution was diffused. Cultural features of this period include agricoltural settlement, animals domestication, the growing of cereals, weaving and clay firing for food potteries. The Ceramic findings, often with raw decorations of shell edges, witness man's presence along the Mediterranean coasts and particularly in many Italian sites (Smith, 1974). Populations coming from the East reached the coasts after 6,000 B.P. and brought new hydraulic technologies, which had allowed the exploitation and cropping of the deltaic plains in Mesopotamia and Egypt (Toynbee, 1965). Some archaeological evidences of hydraulic works in the vicinities of Rome confirm the farming expansion in coastal lowlands and by the river mouths, while for some areas in the southern Adriatic there is evidence of new commercial activities based on timber, flint and perhaps pottery. Between the XIII and the XI century B.C. new migrations from the Mediterranean basin reached the Italian coasts through land and sea.

---

* Researcher, Istituto di Geografia, Università di Bologna, Via S. Giacomo n. 3, 40126 Bologna, Italy.

Figure 1.   Italian administrative regions.

The latter regarded particularly the southern Adriatic coast with flows from the Balkans, originating hundreds of villages. Archaeological findings prove an increased trend of settling which results in fortified villages. New immigrants more developed from the technical viewpoint, forced pre-existing settled groups to move towards the hilly inside, and there was therefore the first case of alternation and settlement castling for defence purposes.

Starting from the IX-VIII century B.C. the middle Tyrrhenian coast experienced the strong influence of the Etrurian civilization. The sea and the coastal lands were the reasons for the growth to power but also for the following decadence of this people, whose origin is not well known yet. The Etrurians succeeded in developing and improving all those techniques which were heritage of the peoples settled earlier, as fisheries, commercial sailing, coastal agricolture and settlings on the first rises behind the coast (Delano Smith, 1979; Bianchi, 1985). Villages became towns, well connected to landing places which, situated near to coves or headlands, grew in importance, thus becoming commercial ports (Schmiedt, 1970). Etrurian's economic activities were at first oriented mainly towards the sea, and only later they turned landwards, expanding influence and controlling wide areas. In this way, a network of centers was originated, on a coastal strip about 30 km wide and extended from the Arno to the Tiber (fig. 2).

Between the V and IV century B.C. at least 750,000 people lived in this area with a density which reached 100 inhabitants/square km (Lattanzi, 1974). The eight main towns, located at some 10 km from the sea, totalled about 150,000 people. North-wards along the Tuscany coast, the settlement fitted to the particular natural conditions and tended to become less frequent, in an area where marshes and uncontrolled river mouths dominate. The hydraulic regimen of these areas begins to be negatively affected by deforestation, actively promoted by the Etrurians. The light settlement of central-northern Etruria privileged the hills dominating river mouths, coves and rises near coastal lakes. The coastal environment complexity gave rise to original solutions: here the only Etrurian town on the coast - Populonia - was founded, at the end of a promontory (Schmiedt, 1970). Its maritime character comes from the remarkable economic, commercial and strategic importance of the iron production developed here.

From the V century B.C. the decadence of Etrurian towns began, as they were unable to keep the control of Tyrrhenian Sea and to defend their commercial ports which were the source of their richness and power (Bianchi, 1985). The settlement structure and the relatively high densities which had characterized the Etrurian Tyrrhenian coast gradually disappeared, without being replaced by a similarly strong civilization. The loss of the Tyrrhenian hegemony forced the Etrurians to privilege the Po area - and therefore the facing on the Adriatic Sea - where they were already present since the IX century with the town of Felsina (Bologna) in the center of an intensively farmed lowland (Mansuelli-Scarani, 1961). A set of important towns and ports became the connection among the Eastern Mediterranean Sea and the continental Europe. The town of Spina, founded on a Po branch, was important, and its necropolis - nowadays about 8 km from the sea because of siltation - include about 4,000 graves. The prosperity period of the Adriatic Etruria was short: the dynamism of the Adriatic lowlands interested by important river mouths in continuous progradation and the flows of Celtic populations dismountled from the IV B.C. Etruscan towns and commerces (Alfieri-Arias, 1960).

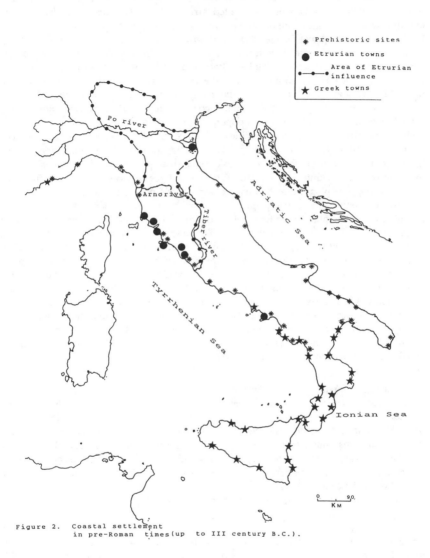

Figure 2. Coastal settlement
in pre-Roman times(up to III century B.C.).

The conditions that in the X century B.C. had started the Phoenician expansion in the Mediterranean Sea were again present two centuries later with the Greeks. The remarkable population growth, the limited size of the "city-states" and the frequent conflicts among them, the unfavourable environment of the inner lands, the search for landing places to improve the commercial network, were all factors that caused a strong push towards the western Mediterranean Sea. The Greek colons found favourable conditions along the coasts of Southern Italy and Sicily for their central position with respect to the Mediterranean basin. After the first settlement, in the Isle of Ischia and related to the iron trade with Etruria, later ones were mainly concentrated along the Ionian, Sicilian and Southern Tyrrhenian coast. A few landing places were already settled by small groups of indigenous population, usually on the first hills, and employed with sheep-rearing and farming activities, which regarded the coastal lowlands to. The urban culture of the Greeks was clearly superior to the one of the local populations, which mostly took shelter in the most inaccessible inner areas, and were partially enslaved by the newcomers, becoming useful laborforce. The Greek towns, differently from the Etrurian ones, were placed directly on the coast, in good position for controlling maritime routes. This first generation was soon followed by the one of towns situated in the center of wide low coastal plains with favourable conditions for farming to meet the demand of an increasing population (Schmiedt, 1970). The towns of the first type gave often origin to those of the second type, with a resulting short-range migration. Archaeological findings show that the farming land was subdivided in regular parcels, so as to favour a dense rural settlement. The coastal occupation by Greek colons also extended to the Adriatic coasts and the trading of the Greeks widely interested the area. A precise evaluation of Greek coastal settlement looks rather difficult; however the literary sources and archaeological researches have supplied elements for reliable estimations. It is therefore deemed that the population of the main centers of the Magna Grecia reached 100,000 inhabitants, ranging from 15,000 and 40,000 in many others, to group up to 500,000 people in about fifteen colonies (Guzzo, 1982).

The maritime supremacy in the Tyrrhenian Sea, and therefore the security of coastal towns, became a reason of conflicts between Phoenician-Carthaginians, Etrurians and Greeks. After a first stage, during which the first two were allied and defeated the Greeks, in the V century B.C. the towns of the Magna Grecia defeated first the Carthaginians and then the Etrurians, thus pursuing the military and commercial supremacy. Successively populations living in inner areas of the Italian peninsula, mainly devoted to sheep-rearing, started to push towards the coast, because of a strong population growth. Starting from the end of the IV century this led to a gradual military or pacific conquest of many towns that in any case kept a good vitality and a continuity in their population.

The expansion process of the Roman power in the whole peninsula starts from the coasts in the IV century B.C. The first colonies founded on the coast were military strongholds (coloniae maritimae), usually garrisoned by three hundreds colonist-soldiers. A network of strongholds along the coast, from the Tiber mouth to the Circeo promontory, formed a defensive line of the Pontine lowlands (Schmiedt, 1970). Later on the Roman expansion was directed towards south along the coast, using as penetration path the Via Appia (312 B.C.). To the North, Etruscan coastal towns were overwhelmed by the Romans because of their coastal military supremacy. In fact Roman presence along the Tyrrhenian coast

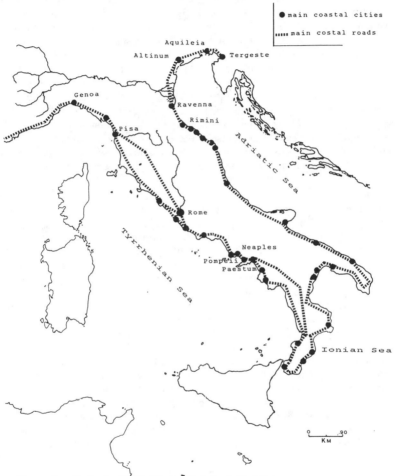

Figure 3. Italy in Roman times (II B.C. — IV A.D.)

was initially a true military action. The basic episodes of this action were the foundation of about ten coloniae maritimae (aligned on the coast north of the Tiber) starting from the III century B.C. and the beginning, in the same period, of the works for construction of the Via Aurelia. On the Adriatic coasts the Roman action had the same characters: only after the establishment of military settlements the colonization was widened with agricolture, roads construction and the development of coastal centers, later on important towns: Aquileia, Trieste, Ravenna, Rimini (fig. 3). With the establishment of a dense network of colonies along the Tyrrhenian coasts Rome was able to move to the conquest of new territories towards north and south. The coastal strongholds offered good supporting points to the Roman armies and after the Punic Wars (III century) Rome had extended its control on all the most important peninsular coastlands. The war destructions and the forced absence of farmers from the land to serve in the Roman legions brought to the decadence of agriculture based on the small and middle land estates resulting in some central and southern areas in the diffusion of the latifundium, with slave labor for cereal production and rearing. The following tendency to agglomeration of the rural population led to the gradual decrease of the sparse settlement and to the abandonment of drainage and hydraulic regulation works in coastal lowlands, which along the Etrurian and Latian coast up to the Circeo were partly transformed into marshes (Sereni, 1972; Pratesi, 1985).

From the mid part of the III century B.C. the Italian peninsula recorded a remarkable population growth. The population, from 4 or 5 millions (225 B.C.) people, exceeded 7 millions people at the time of the census of 28 B.C. (Bellettini, 1973). The Tyrrhenian coasts of central Italy were not affected by this increase, as long coast stretches turned into marshes and waste lands, allocated to wild grazing of cattle and herd. In the II century B.C. the southern Latian coast, between the Tiber and the Circeo, was marshy and depopulated; this caused deportations of populations from Campania (Schmiedt, 1970). Along the Etrurian coast the decay of coastal centers corresponded in time to the latifundium farming expansion and, between the V and III century B.C., to a malaria recrudescence (Delano Smith, 1979). The malaric fever was very common in the coastal stretch from the Arno mouth to the Pontine lowlands around 200 B.C. To combat this, in 160 B.C. a wide reclamation and re-population action of the coast south of Rome was started. Julius Caesar to (59 B.C.) tried to encourage the coastal settlement and productive activities, and this action went on in the first centuries of the empire. The results however did not bring substantial changes in the population distribution along the coasts. In the age of Augustus (28 B.C. - 14 A.D.) the most populated coastal regions were Liguria and Campania on the Tyrrhenian coast, Marche - where a limited farming activity had survived - and the territories near Ravenna, Aquileia and Trieste on the Adriatic coast. With the following period of peace some of the coastal towns of Magna Grecia gradually recovered from decadence and depopulation which had affected them during the first years of the Roman conquest (Guzzo, 1982). The most developed and prosperous areas were along the Campania coasts, where large commercial centers flourished (Pozzuoli, Naples, Ercolano, Pompeii, Paestum). The Campania coast became the favourite residence for the Roman aristocracy and the emperors themselves, as the findings of beautiful villas prove. Where the coast was healthy luxury buildings flourished, often surrounded by prosperous farm estates. Many of these villas were supplied with large tanks connected to the sea for fish breeding (Schmiedt, 1972). Along the coasts, the commercial activities thrived, because of the building expansion of the towns and especially of Rome. The marbles of the Tuscany quarries, embarked in the port of Luna, sailed along the Tyrrhenian coast, then along the Tiber river up to the port of Rome

(Dolci, 1987). Timber to - transported to Rome from the woods of the northern Appennines, the Rhaetian Alps and the Calabrian mountains - followed a maritime course. Deforestation brought to hydraulic disorder process of some coastal areas and their abandonment. The political and economical decadence of the empire, the slave latifundium extension, malaria recrudescence and climatic changes, - which led to a sea level increase (Bird-Fabbri, 1983) - caused from the Roman power decadence (IV-V century A.D.) a remarkable population decrease in most of Italian low coastlands, enphasizing the effects of a general population decrease due to epidemics, famines and barbarian invasions. In 400 A.D. in what was called Campania felix, about 14,000 hectares were marshy and abandoned because of lack of labor; the same for wide cultivated areas on the Adriatic and Ionian coasts (Luzzatto, 1958). Climate changes encouraged the degradation and depopulation of coastal areas; the Barbarian kings themselves, replacing the Roman power, were forced to exempt from taxation wide unproductive land extensions (Pratesi, 1985).

The gradual dissolution of the Roman power brought to deep changes in the Italian political, economical and social structure: as a matter of fact a political division and instability, lasting up to the formation of a unified nation (1861). There is a first stage of farming decadence, especially in the lowlands and a global reduction of the productive commercial activities. People tended to privilege annucleated settlement with walls and, when possible, located in elevated place (Klapisch-Zuber, 1972). The population increase in the mountain areas from this period up to the start of present century involved an extended deforesting and farming along slopes with consequent alterations of the river courses.

The population growth of the Roman age, which had reached 8 millions inhabitants, shows a sudden inversion, and was halved between the VII and the VIII century A.D. The coastal areas are as well interested by this process. As a matter of fact there are many evidences of the settlement and coastal communication decadence in areas once densely populated and intensely farmed, where the only activity became the cattle wild grazing. This general trend shows differentiations in quality and quantity level between northern and central-southern Italy. If, indeed, devastations, depopulation, economic decline and the extension of marshy areas involve almost homogeneously the whole peninsula, it is to be noted on a more local base destruction of the coastal towns in Liguria and in the Northern Adriatic; the increasing pressure of piracy forcing settlement withdrawing and castling along the central and southern Adriatic and Tyrrhenian Seas; the extension of marshes in coastal lowlands of Tuscany, Latium, Campania, Calabria and Apulia.

After the XI century, evident signs of recovery can be found in central and northern Italy, with population increase up to the XIII century (Bellettini, 1973). In fact, many monasteries and abbeys had been carrying for centuries hydraulic regulation works and coastal land farming both on the Adriatic and Tyrrhenian coasts. Further initiatives followed in the centuries on part of main towns, where the population growth was remarkable. The development of economic activities led to an increase in tradings. Even if in the previous centuries some coastal centers - above all those under the Byzantines rule - had mantained connections in the Mediterranean, from the X-XI century new important ports appear on the scene. On the Adriatic coast the growth of Venice and a series of less important landing places in the middle part begins, while in the south Bari is always the most important. On the Tyrrhenian coast, after the XI century, besides the Byzantine port of Amalfi there are Pisa and Genoa. Italian maritime cities have their definite achievement with their participation to the Crusades. The cooperation to the Christian armies are rewarded by granting important commercial privileges which ensure a monopoly on the trading in the Mediterranean (Luzzatto, 1958). In the south of Italy, and in some areas of the center, still in the XIV and in XV centuries the depopulation of the coastal lowlands is remarkable, reaching about 1/3 of the centers of the reign of Naples and losses much higher than 50% of the population along the Tuscany coast (Jones, 1976). In these areas the settlement is still limited to areas at an elevation of 300-400 m while the presence of man in the lowlands is mainly limited to sheperds and the occupants of the watch towers, more and more numerous along the coast to control piracy and blunder. The discontinuity between the inner territories, where population and activities are concentrated, and the coast, transformed into marginal land, is clearly shown by literary documentations and statistical data. The maritime city-state of Amalfi itself was abandoned in the XIV century by most of its population because of continuous attacks (Epifanio, 1930). The towns of the "Terra d'Otranto" (Apulia) were so depopulated in the half of the V century to force the Government to grant large fiscal and judiciary privileges to all people moving to Lecce or Brindisi. The low population density of the coastal towns was one of the reasons allowing the Turks to conquer Otranto in 1480 and explaining why the local powers needed so long a time to take again the full control of those areas (Figliuolo, 1985).

The economic and demographic growth in the X-XIII centuries does not have a steady trend but a continuous alternation of positive and negative stages. There are, as a matter of fact, frequent crises due both to the conflicts between different cities and the numberless epidemics and plagues on dense urban population. Pisa is a clear example of this trend: after having reached the highest economic and demographic stage with 25,000 inhabitants in the second half of the XIII century, declined after a major defeat by Genoa and at the half of the XV century the population was under 9,000 inhabitants.

List of References

Alfieri, N.; Arias, P.E.: Spina. Guida al museo archeologico. Sansoni, Firenze 1960.

Bellettini, A.: La popolazione italiana dall'inizio dell'era volgare ai giorni nostri. Valutazione e tendenze. In: Storia d'Italia, I Documenti, 1, pp. 489-536. Einaudi, Torino 1973.

Bianchi, G.M.: Il mondo storico degli Etruschi. Supplemento a L'Universo 65, 5 (1985).

Bird, E.C.F.; Fabbri, P.: Archeological evidence of coastline changes illustrated with reference to Latium, Italy. In: Colloques internationaux C.N.R.S. Déplacements des lignes de rivage en Méditérranée, pp. 107-113. Paris 1987.

Dolci, E.: I marmi della Colonna Traiana. Deputazione di storia patria per le antiche province modenesi, Atti e Memorie 11, 10, 46-65 (1987).

Epifanio, V.: Le fonti più importanti per lo studio degli spostamenti di popolazione meridionale nel secolo XIV. In: Atti del XI Congr. Geogr. It., v. II, pp. 309-317. Napoli 1930.

Delano Smith, C.: Western Mediterranean Europa. Academic Press, London 1979.

Figliuolo, B.: Il terremoto napoletano del 1456. Quaderni Storici 60, 3, 771-809 (1985).

Guzzo, P.G.: Le città scomparse della Magna Grecia. Newton Compton, Roma 1982.

Klapish-Zuber, C.: Villaggi abbandonati. In: Storia d'Italia, I Documenti, I, pp. 311-369. Einaudi, Torino 1973.

Jones, P.: L'Italia. In: Storia Economica Cambridge, I, pp. 412-526. Einaudi, Torino 1976.

Lattanzi, M.S.: Le antiche città dell'Etruria: saggio di Geografia Urbana. Pubbl. n. 3 dell'Ist. di Geografia, Firenze 1974.

Luzzatto, G.: Breve storia economica dell'Italia medievale. Einaudi, Torino 1958.

Mansuelli, G.A.; Scarani, R.: L'Emilia prima dei Romani. Il Saggiatore, Milano 1961.

Pratesi, F.: Gli ambienti naturali e l'equilibrio ecologico. In: Storia d'Italia, Annali, 8, pp. 53-162. Einaudi, Torino 1985.

Radmilli, A.M.: Guida alla preistoria italiana. Sansoni, Firenze 1978.

Schmiedt, G. (ed.): Atlante aerofotografico delle sedi umane in Italia. Note introduttive. I.G.M., Firenze 1970.

Schmiedt, G. (ed.): Il livello antico del mar Tirreno. Testimonianze dei resti archeologici. Olschki, Firenze 1972.

Sereni, E., Agricoltura e mondo rurale. In: Storia d'Italia. I caratteri originali, pp. 136-255. Einaudi, Torino 1972.

Smith, C.T.: Geografia storica d'Europa. Dalla preistoria al XIX secolo. Laterza, Bari 1974.

Toynbee, A.J.: Nuove esigenze e opportunità economiche nell'Italia peninsulare e nella cisalpina dopo la guerra annibalica. In: Capogrossi Colognesi, L.(ed.): L'agricoltura romana. Guida storica e critica. Laterza, Bari 1982.

Historical Evolution of the Coastal Settlement
in Italy: Modern Times

Achille Lodovisi[*]

Abstract

This contribution is aimed to follow the coastal populating development in Italy (isles excluded) in the modern and contemporary age. The man presence privileged - in ancient time - high coasts, and only later the low ones as well (fig. 1). These have a more dynamic coastal populating in the modern age, alternating growing and decreasing due to the complex historical and economic happenings of the Italian peninsula.

It is possible to analyse the people concentration along the coast from a quantity viewpoint only having homogeneous and sufficiently reliable statistical data: in Italy these conditions are present only after the Unification (1861). From the half of the XV century to 1861 there are statistical data, more and more numerous and precise, but they are not based on homogeneous criteria and therefore they cannot always be compared.

After the demographic setback of the XIV century, the following century brings a slow recovery. Coastal areas underwent in that period, after centuries of abandonment, large reclamation schemes. In 1505 the Republic of Venice created the "Collegio delle Acque" (Water Council), an agency for the control of rivers flowing into the lagoon. This measure regarded not only indispensable interventions against the siltation of lagoon but also the management of inland areas. In the XVI century more than 15,000 hectares out of the 30,000 of marshlands were reclaimed (Romano, 1971). Along the southern Adriatic coasts important reclamation schemes had been started from the XIV century. But they were isolated for a long time: all of the Ionian and the Calabrian Tyrrhenian coasts up to Salerno were still depopulated, infested by malaria and pirates. This was a sort of "no-man's-land", unsafe even in ports and therefore avoided by maritime trading. In the XVI century the corn from Apulia, for the increasing population in Naples, reached this city only by land (Giannetti, 1985). In 1532 the Spanish government in Naples decided to revaluate the coast between Naples and Rome, for military and political reasons. The ancient Roman road along coast was reactivated, assigned to mail service and preferred to the inland itinerary. This brought to the completion of the road works, reclamation and new settlements in previously abandoned areas. The road and the new settlements were protected against the piracy by building watchtowers along the coast. Reclamation schemes were also started in the Papal State, where Pope Sisto V fostered the first hydraulic regulation works in the Pontine Marshes (Nicolaj, 1984).

---

* Researcher, S.G.A. (Storia, Geofisica e Ambiente), Via Bellombra n. 24/2, 40136 Bologna - Italy.

Figure 1.   Italian administrative regions.

In the Grand Duchy of Tuscany, to relaunch the populating and the agriculture, the first interventions on rivers were started with the aim of settling costal areas, and a series of edicts limited, in the countryside of Pisa, diffusion of grazing, fostering instead the peasant immigration from the nearby Liguria, which was densely populated (Klapish-Zuber, 1973). In the XVI century there was an intensification of the deforestation and agricoltural settlement in the hills, which resulted in deterioration of the hydraulic regime of water courses flowing into the coastal lowlands. Therefore there was a malaria uprise along coasts still unreclaimed. Malaria was so lethal among the thousands of settlers that, at the end of the XVI century, people moved to the coasts from overpopulated mountainous areas, only as a result of the fiscal and land grants (Braudel, 1976).

The agricoltural revaluation of the coastal lowlands of Tuscany was above all due to the need of increasing the cereal production and developing the military and commercial presence of the Grand Duchy in the central Tyrrhenian basin. At the end of the XVI century these targets were indeed only partially reached. The only real success was the large development of the town of Leghorn and of its port, declared "free port" at the half of the XVI century. The immigration of Jewish merchants, burglars and sailors from all parts of the Mediterranean, attracted by the tolerant policy of the Grand Dukes, helped the success of the town, where up to the end of the XV century nobody had wanted to live because of the unhealthy environment (Day, 1973; Braudel, 1976).

Reclamation schemes of the XVI century had on the whole poor results. The high cost of hydraulic works burdened heavily on budgets already loaded by military expenses. Farming techniques were obsolete and there still were bonds imposed by land rules of a feudal type. Therefore the plans of settlement of a dense farming population along coast did not succeed. At the end of the XVI century the stretches of populated coast were the same as two centuries before: the Ligurian coast, the gulf of Naples and Apulia between Bari and Brindisi; low coasts were mainly deserted. From 1522 pyrate raids got to be more frequent, as following to the fall of Rhodes, the Turkish pressure was closer to Italian coasts. The danger was so serious to force the Spanish Viceroys to allocate substancial resources of the reign of Naples in the building of hundreds of coastal watchtowers. A military garrison line was created along all of the southern coast. The defence structure was not only against piracy but also against bandits in the poor and depopulated coastal villages where they lived. In 1585 the army of the Reign of Naples received the order to destroy all villages with a population under 100 inhabitants, and to deport them in larger and fortified centers (Klapish-Zuber, 1973). Even if data are not always reliable, in Naples the population increased from 60,000 in the XIV century to 210,000 in 1547, to reach 280,000 at the end of the XVI century. In Venice the increase was from 130,000 (1338) to 190,000 in the XV century, to exceed 180,000 in 1563. Rome reached 55,000 inhabitants in the early XVI century then to decrease again. Florence and Genoa, although economically important, only reached about 60,000 inhabitants at the half of the XVI century. Genoa's growth in this period should be related to the financial and commercial influence of the Spanish Empire, as the city was home to many banks and the diffusion center towards the European markets of silver coming from the Americas. At the end of the XVI century there were the first signs of the general economical crisis which continued up to the early XVIII century. Beside this long period of economical stagnation, also linked to the progressive shifting of the

European commercial core from the Mediterranean to the North Sea, there were also two serious epidemics (1630-1631, 1656-1657) and repeated famines. At the end of the XVII century, with the exception of Leghorn, all coastal cities suffered a demographic setback and the number of inhabitants was exactly the same as one century before, about 12 millions (Bellettini, 1973; Del Panta, 1980). Most of the Italian coastlands experienced these negative influences, and often abandonment.

Between the XVII and XVIII century there were differentiated population trends in the various areas of the peninsula. The Northern Italy, between 1650 and 1700, had a growth over 30%. The Central Italy was stationary, while in the peninsular area of the reign of Naples, despite the plague in 1656, there was an increase by 16% in the second half of the XVII century (Bellettini, 1979). Italy on the whole experienced the population expansion later than the other European countries in the XVII century. The coastal population trend in these centuries is directly influenced and connected to the described general trends. For example, in the Sorrento peninsula (south of Naples), the population, after the very high mortality of the plague in 1656, started slowly but steadily to increase: from about 70,000 inhabitants at the end of the XVII century to 145,000 in 1821. A population doubling in about 150 years agrees with the general trend in the whole of Italy. The coasts with good environmental conditions followed the general population trend, while coastal belts that had been depopulated long ahead, remained in the same state (Di Vittorio, 1977). The population increase in the inland areas led on one hand to a further expansion of the slope cultivations, with negative effects on the hydraulic regimen of the rivers flowing into the coastal lowlands, and on the other hand to increasing seasonal migrations of the mountain population. At the end of the XVIII century tens of thousands of highlanders were migrating towards the lowlands of the Roman and Tuscan countryside to harvest and thresh the corn, and were often affected by malarial fevers; once ended the works, peasants abandoned the lands that in winter only housed sheep which were moved to different pastures (Da Molin, 1980; Celli, 1984; Nicolaj, 1984).

As it already happened about two centuries before, in the last decades of the XVIII century public interventions for coastal land reclamation took place. Works were carried out in the Tuscan coast, south of Leghorn, and lasted for all the following century. In Tuscany these works had encouraging results with the reclamation of 8,700 hectares, so that the population in Maremma increased, thus inverting a consolidated depopulation trend (Bellettini, 1980). Grosseto had, at the half of the XVIII century, 648 inhabitants, and after a century they went up to 2,331. Not always however the results were lasting and extended: for example the foundation of new centers at the end of the XVIII century in Apulia did not lead to an immediate settlement in nearby territories. Even in the Pontine Marshes reclamation schemes started by pope Pio VI (1777) were hindered by the land structure, mainly formed by cereal and grazing latifundium, where the exploitation of marshy areas and coastal bushes was part of the economy of large estates. The land register of 1783 pointed out as a quarter of the whole Roman plain was owned by only three owners (Cacherano di Bircherasio, 1984). The coastal areas remained therefore depopulated, with an average density that in a 100-year time (1701-1811) increses from four to two inhabitants per sq\km. (Schiavoni-Sonnino, 1984). Ostia, the ancient port of Rome, was completely depopulated for most of the XVIII century. The stagnation of Latium, in comparison with the average Italian growth, is essentially due to losses in the coastal areas: at the end of the century, Cerveteri, the village born on the ruins of the Etrurian Caere and which had had up to 30,000 inhabitants, did not have more than 250. In the first years of the XIX century a survey conducted by the Napoleonic Government on the state of the Roman departments confirmed the abandonment and depopulation of the Roman countryside and coast (De Felice, 1968). The results of the Pontine reclamations, suspended in 1799, were as a whole quite poor, even if some thousands of hectares were turned to cultivation again (Bevilacqua - Rossi-Doria, 1984).

The southern Italian coasts were desolated as well: at the end of the XVIII century the coastal areas north and south of Naples, the low coasts of the Ionian and Tyrrhenian Calabria, of Basilicata and most of the Adriatic coast of Apulia were more or less depopulated. Out of a total of 4,800,000 inhabitants, 22% lived in built-up areas along the coast stretch which was about 2,000 km long, but, excluding the population of Naples, only 14% lived in the coastal areas which were a belt of ponds and marshes (Galanti, 1969; Filangieri, 1980). The Napoleonic government, in the first years of the XIX century, was promoter of an abolition policy for the feudal structure still burdening the land rule, and at the same time some coastal reclamation interventions were started, going on even after the Restoration (1814) of the previous regimes. In 1861 the new Italian state received as a heritage from the Reign of Naples 17 reclamation interventions, all in progress and in uncertain conditions (Grasselli Lussana, 1983). The situation in the period of the national unification (1861) was generally the same as in previous centuries: a study of military geography of 1859 depicts low coasts as generally abandoned and depopulated. These coasts were substantially an efficient defensive line preventing or obstructing the attacks of a potential invader (Mezzacapo, 1859). The defensive function was therefore the only remarkable element which, after centuries of different events the coastal areas still had.

Since the political unification of Italy (1861) the coastal population analysis has sufficiently homogeneous and reliable statistical data for evaluations from a quantitative viewpoint. At the same time, with a central administrative structure, the interventions for coastal areas went under the national legislation. The analysis of homogeneous statistical data, starting from 1871, has been made on the basis of the first level administrative districts (Comuni) facing the sea. In the quite frequent case of districts with numerous population settled at a remarkable distance from the sea only the really coastal one, that is evidently connected to the sea, was considered. So the enclosed data refer directly, in a sufficiently reliable way, to the populating development in the "coastal zone".

This period is characterized by a trend of progressive concentration of inhabitants and activities along coasts. Out of the total of the Italian population, the coastal-residing portion shifts from 10% (1871) to 14.6% (1981), with a peak of 14.9% (1971) (fig. 3). The essential reasons are to be found in reclamation and farm evaluation interventions; in the construction of railways and roads along coasts; in the formation of industrial structures near the ports, and last but not least, in tourism development.

The reclamation interventions concerning the coastal areas for a period of about 90 years (1880-1970) have been fostered by the central government, with the aim of fighting malaria and increasing the value of large estates (1882-1920) and later to complete land

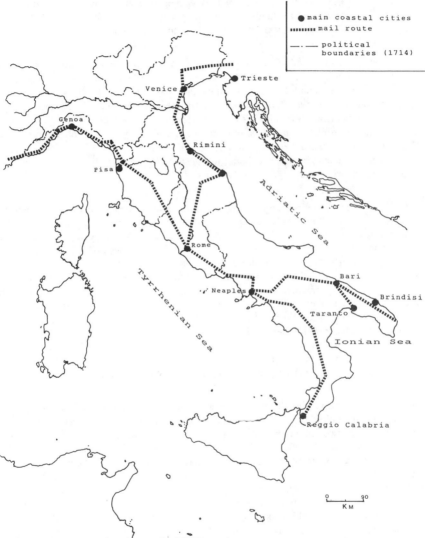

Figure 2. Italy in the early XVIII century.

farming utilization. After World War II reclamation schemes started again in compliance with the "land reform", aimed to facilitate land ownership by a large number of peasants, forming small family farms. In the first period coastal areas in Veneto, Emilia, Apulia, Basilicata and Campania were reclaimed. Between 1920 and 1940 special efforts had been made along coastal lowlands in Latium, Tuscany, Calabria and Veneto. After the war reclamation works mainly concerned Adriatic and Ionian coasts.

The construction of a railway network was one of the essential elements for the real unification of the Italy. From about 1,800 km operating in 1860 - none along the coasts - in 1880 there were about 10,000, and, more important, there were railways parallel to most of coastal stretches. Railway junctions in the deserted coastal lowlands became centers of settlements. Migration flows that from the last decades of the XIX century concerned almost all Italian coasts, mainly originated from inland mountainous areas. The attraction of coastal plains was due to availability of lands for a commercial agriculture; to better standards of living; to the increasing availability of labour demand due to the expansion of the-agricoltural sectors.

Increase rates of coastal population have been higher than the national average, with the only exception of the last analyzed period (1971-1981), during which the coastal data (+2.7%) are lower than the national average (+4.7%) (fig. 4). The peaks for the coastal population growth are to be found between 1901-1921 (+12.1%) and 1951-1961 (+13.2%), when the values are more than doubled in comparison with the national average (+5.7%). For the first interval the reasons may be the initial results of the reclamations, the completion of the coastal communication network, the expansion of the industrial activities - especially in the coastal belts of Friuli, of Liguria and Tuscany - and in the effects of World War I, which drove many peasants away from the countryside, thus breaking deeply the traditional rural society. For the second period it must be noted the rural depopulation, which reaches the highest values, fostering the immigration in the town centers. This latter makes up about 80% of the town expansion (+23%) and is related to the reconstruction following World War II.

Analyzing by regions (fig. 5), the Tyrrhenian coast shows in the whole surveyed period, the highest population increase: which is not due to continuous settlement but mainly to the presence of two large cities as Genoa and Naples. The development of these two urban areas was mainly influenced by governmental industrial investments, from the last decade of the XIX century. At the same time in this coast there was the slowest increase rate, in comparison to the other two, even with a sort of stagnation in the decade 1971-1981 (+1.1%) (fig. 4), due to saturation and decline in the Ligurian urban area and to setback in the Naples area. The regional population on the coast (fig. 5) confirms these data: Liguria (no. 10) and Campania (no. 13) have a decrease in coastal population that in the last decade varies respectively from 80.4% and 41% to 79.1% and 38.7%. Two more Tyrrhenian regions, Latium (no. 12) and Tuscany (no. 11) record instead a standstill in coastal population in comparison to the global one. This slowing down is present also in the northern Adriatic where coastal stretches of Friuli (no. 1) and Veneto (no. 2) progressively decrease their population in relation with the demographic setback in Trieste and Venice. Middle Adriatic regions record the most remarkable and steady population along the coast. In Emilia (no. 3), Marche (no. 4), Abruzzi (no. 5) and Molise (no. 6) the coastal area has become, in a few decades, a densely populated one with numerous of productive activities, stimulated by the presence of a plain and efficient accessibility. This development, unlikely the one along the Tyrrhenian front, starts after World War II and is mainly all based on local economic resources.

Tourism has surely helped the increase in value of the Italian coasts, but in building development than in population. Contrasting population trends of the coastal areas widely interested by tourism confirm this, as some of them even show a decrease of population along coast or at least a slower growth than in inland areas.

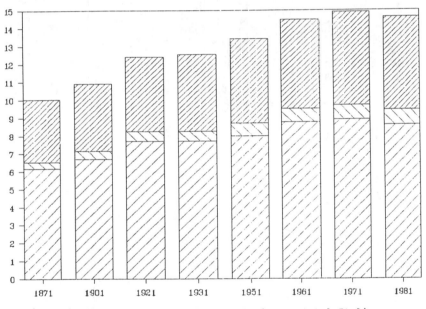

Figure 3. Percentage of coastal population on total Italian population.

▨ Tyrrhenian front   ◹ Ionian front   ▨ Adriatic front

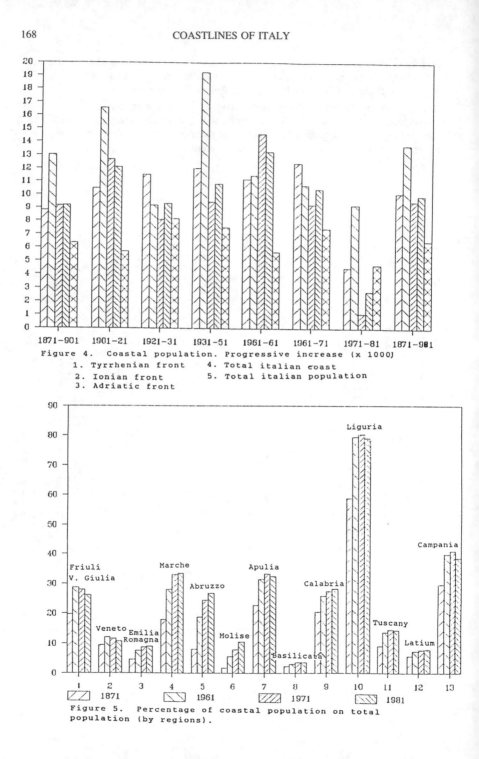

Figure 4. Coastal population. Progressive increase (x 1000)

1. Tyrrhenian front   4. Total italian coast
2. Ionian front   5. Total italian population
3. Adriatic front

Figure 5. Percentage of coastal population on total population (by regions).

List of References

Bellettini, A.: La popolazione italiana dall'inizio dell'era volgare ai giorni nostri. Valutazione e tendenze. In: Storia d'Italia, I Documenti, 1, pp. 489-536. Einaudi, Torino 1973.

Bellettini, A.: L'evoluzione demografica dell'Italia nel quadro europeo del Settecento: analogie e particolarità. In: S.I.D.E.S., La popolazione italiana nel Settecento, pp. 13-70. Clueb, Bologna 1980.

Bevilacqua, P.; Rossi Doria, M. (eds.): Le bonifiche in Italia dal '700 ad oggi. Laterza, Bari 1984.

Braudel, F., Civiltà ed imperi del Mediterraneo nell'età di Filippo II. Einaudi, Torino 1976.

Cacherano di Bicherasio, G.F.M.: Il ripopolamento dell'agro romano. In: Bevilacqua, P.; Rossi Doria, M. (eds.): Le bonifiche in Italia dal '700 ad oggi, pp. 132-137. Laterza, Bari 1984.

Celli, A.: Contadini nella campagna romana. In: Bevilacqua, P.; Rossi Doria, M. (eds.): Le bonifiche in Italia dal '700 ad oggi, pp. 234-243. Laterza, Bari 1984.

Da Molin, G.: Mobilità dei contadini pugliesi tra fine '600 e primo '800. In: S.I.D.E.S., La popolazione italiana nel Settecento, pp. 435-476. Clueb, Bologna 1980.

Day, J.: Strade e vie di comunicazione. In: Storia d'Italia, I Documenti, 1, pp. 89-127. Einaudi, Torino 1973.

De Felice, R.: L'Inchiesta napoleonica per i Dipartimenti romani (1809-1810). Rassegna degli Archivi di Stato 28, 67-102 (1968).

Del Panta, L.: Le epidemie nella storia demografica italiana (secoli XIV-XIX). Loesher, Torino 1980.

Di Vittorio, A.: Le acque continentali e le attività umane nel Mezzogiorno d'Italia nei secoli XVIII e XIX. In: Atti del XXII Congr. Geogr. It., v. II, t. I, pp. 41-70. Napoli 1977.

Filangieri, A.: Territorio e popolazione nell'italia meridionale. Evoluzione storica. F. Angeli, Milano 1980.

Galanti, G.M.: Della descrizione geografica e politica delle Sicilie. E.S.I., Napoli 1969.

Giannetti, A.: La strada dalla città al territorio: la riorganizzazione spaziale nel Regno di Napoli nel Cinquecento. In : Storia d'Italia, Annali, 8, pp. 243-272. Einaudi, Torino 1985.

Grasselli Lussana, E.: L'attività di bonifica elemento di modificazione del paesaggio. In: Atti del XXII Congr. Geogr. It., v. II, t. III, pp. 234-249. Catania 1983.

Klapish-Zuber, C.: Villaggi abbandonati. Storia d'Italia, I Documenti, I, pp. 311-369. Einaudi, Torino 1973.

Mezzacapo, L. & C.: Studj topografici e strategici su l'Italia. Vallardi, Milano 1859.

Nicolaj, N.M.: La bonifica pontificia delle paludi pontine. In: Bevilacqua, P.; Rossi Doria, M. (eds.): Le bonifiche in Italia dal '700 ad oggi, pp. 138-150. Laterza, Bari 1984.

Romano, R.: Tra due crisi: l'Italia del Rinascimento. Einaudi, Torino 1971.

Schiavoni, C.; Sonnino, E.: Popolazione e territorio nel Lazio: 1701-1811. In: S.I.D.E.S., La popolazione italiana nel Settecento, pp. 191-226. Clueb, Bologna 1980.

FIRST RESULTS OF A NEW SHORE PROTECTIVE WORK INSTALLED ALONG THE EASTERN ITALIAN COAST

L. Carbognin*, M. Cipriani** and F. Marabini***

The entire Italian coast is presently affected by erosion which has led to a general shoreline regression. This phenomenon is not new but nowadays it is more intense and widespread than in the past, and of great concern to seaside resort areas. In a highly degrading beach, conventional shore protective works (e.g. sea walls, groins, breakwaters) are not adequate to guarantee coastal stability. New types of protective works have been studied and used to oppose the attack of the sea.

The poster shows the first results obtained with a new filter-barrier, called "Ferr-An", patent in Italy, used for the very first time along the eastern Adriatic littoral of Porto Recanati, where it was installed in 1981.

The system, which can be assembled in various ways, consists of three prefabricated concrete struttural elements:
1) equilateral triangular section pile, pointed at the end, and variable length;
2) triangular star-shaped, concrete element;
3) cylindrical spacing bar.

Each pile is driven into the sea bottom for about two-thirds of its length. The star-shaped concrete blocks and the spacers are slipped on the pile. Their number varies according to the depth of the sea bottom.

The pilings are placed at predetermined regular intervals and in rows parallel to each other which, in relation to the prevailing wind, may form a convex angle seawards, as in our case.

Actually it is a dissipator of energy capable of reducing considerably the force of waves and trapping the suspended material from the longshore current.

This barrier is substantially different from the traditional breakwaters because the breaking can be regu-

*   Istituto Studio Dinamica Grandi Masse-CNR, S. Polo 1364
     30125 Venice, Italy
**   Ministero dei Lavori Pubblici, Via Nomentana 2, Rome,
     Italy
*** Istituto Geologia Marina-CNR, Via Zamboni, 65, Bologna,
     Italy

lated, in proportion to protective requirements, by the density of the single elements making up the entire structure.

Moreover, this "Ferr-An" system eliminates the stagnant water which occurs behind traditional breakwaters and the consequent pollution problems by allowing the waves to pass and guaranteeing a continual exchange of water.

Another important advantage for maintaining the beach equilibrium, concerns the longshore transport which results unaltered. In fact, wave motion is only reduced and not cancelled under the lee of the protective work itself. This sediment distribution trend allows in time a uniform shoreline advancing, avoiding the presence of accentuated regression of the coast that is usually found in the beaches adjacent to those protected with traditional breakwaters.

The figures which follow clearly illustrate the Ferr-An shore protective structure and the results which have been so far obtained.

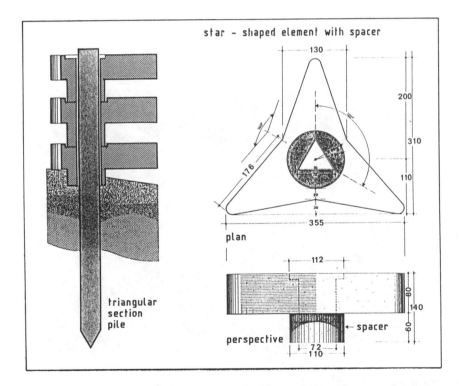

Figure 1. Schematization of a pile with three elements (left); plan and perspective of a single star-shaped concrete element (right).

Figure 2. Installation of the breakwater barrier.

Figure 3. Aerial view of the two parallel rows of the Ferr-An protective work installed near Porto Recanati-Adriatic Sea, Italy. The convex angle seawards is evident.

Figure 4. Close-up of the same barriers in Fig. 3 semi-buried in the sand in 1985, because of the occurred beach accretion.

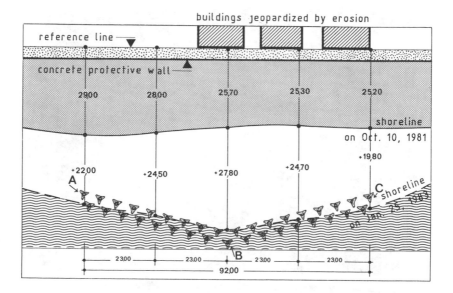

Figure 5. Variation of the backshore occurred during a 15-month period after the placement of the Ferr-An barrier.

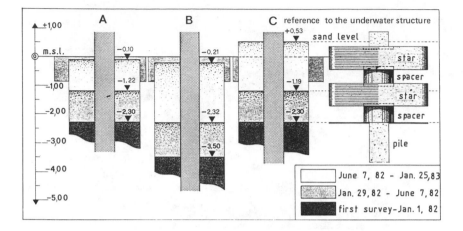

Figure 6.   Amount of natural nourishment at piles A,B,C with respect to m.s.l.   (pile positions indicated in Fig.   5).

Figure 7.   The star-shaped concrete protective work in normal sea and weather conditions.

Figure 8. A close-up of Fig. 7.

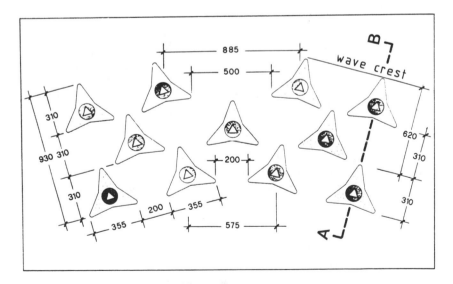

Figure 9. Diagram shows the Ferr-An barrier set-up in the three parallel row version.

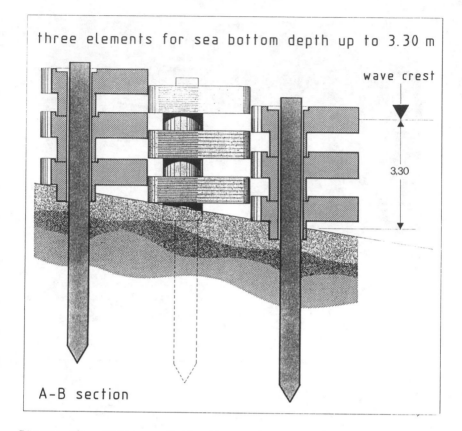

Figure 10.   Diagram of the three elements along the   section
A-B of Fig.   9.

    The authors express their thanks to the Rescoop for
supplying the illustrations for this poster and Mr. G.
Marozzi of the Institute of Marine Geology (Istituto
Geologia Marina-CNR), CNR, Bologna, for his photographic
work.

SUBJECT INDEX
Page number refers to first page of paper.

AUTHOR INDEX
Page number refers to first page of paper.